LET ME TEACH
YOU GOLF
AS I TAUGHT
JACK NICKLAUS

LET ME TEACH YOU GOLF AS I TAUGHT JACK NICKLAUS

Jack Grout

WITH DICK AULTMAN

Illustrated by Jim McQueen

ATHENEUM / SMI

New York   1975

"Everything I've achieved in golf, I've done with techniques taught to me by Jack Grout."

Jack Nicklaus

Foreword

SINCE I STARTED playing golf at age ten, I've had one golf instructor and only one—Jack Grout. The fundamentals that he first pounded into my skull on the practice range at Scioto Country Club, and since then at various places we've traveled and visited together, are still the bedrock of my game. There is no doubt at all that almost everything I've achieved in golf I've done with the techniques taught to me by Jack Grout.

Jack Grout told me what to do when I was ten and he still helps me 25 years later. I make a point to have him check my fundamentals at the start of every golfing season, and thereafter whenever I run into trouble. Also, I try to put my children in his hands as much as I can. He's always willing to help, and he has been that way as long as I've known him.

Jack Grout admits in one breath that the golf swing is a highly complex maneuver—as it is—and then he proceeds to teach it clearly and understandably. He stresses fundamentals, he keeps them to a minimum, and he keeps them simple. I can assure you that the simplicity of Jack's approach is *the* major reason why I've managed to play as well as I have over the years.

Both the simplicity and the completeness of Jack's message come through in this book. You will also find that he never fails to explain to you—as he did to me—the reasons behind his recommendations. This is important in the long run because, as the great Bob Jones once observed, we really don't reach our maximum as players until we understand why we must do what we must do.

Finally, I'd like to say how much I've cherished Jack Grout as a friend as well as a teacher. Along with my parents and my wife, he has been the biggest and surely one of the best influences in my life.

JACK NICKLAUS, 1975

Contents

CHAPTER ONE

Jack and You and Me Make Three

THIS BOOK IS about how you can learn to play golf well and have a lot of fun doing so. Before we start, however, let me quickly tell you a little bit about myself and what has led me to becoming an author.

I suppose when a man gets to be 65 it's time for him to look back on his life and think about the things that made him live it as he has. When I look back I can recall many turning points along the way, but there were two in particular that shaped my destiny.

The first occurred in 1918 when I lived in Oklahoma City. I was eight years old, and I'd decided it was time for me to find out just where my three older brothers went when they left the house in such a hurry every morning.

It was a warm, sunny, summer day and the birds were chirping as I trailed along behind my brothers for about two miles, hiding behind trees and bushes. Finally they came to a fence, jumped over it, and disappeared.

I waited a few minutes and then went and took a peek over the fence. On the other side was the most beautiful sight I'd ever seen. It looked like a huge pasture of lovely green grass and trees and lakes. People were strolling around, hitting little white balls with sticks. Fascinated, I stayed there drinking in the scene for many minutes before I realized that my mother would be looking for me. I ran all the way home.

The next day I went back. I just had to see that pretty scene once again, because at my first sight of one I'd decided that a golf course was the nicest place in the world to be.

The second important day in my life occurred in 1950. By then, beginning by caddieing at the course in Oklahoma City, I'd found out how to play golf. I'd started giving lessons when I was 16. I'd joined the professional tour and competed with all the great American players. I'd learned how to hit high shots and low shots, and shots that curved from left to right and from right to left. I'd learned when to gamble and when to play safe, and how to win and lose. And, finally, I'd become a club professional and now was to settle in Columbus, Ohio, as head pro at the Scioto Country Club.

On that day in Columbus in 1950, I chanced on the way to the club to stop off at a drugstore. There a smiling, heavyset man came up and introduced himself to me. I didn't recognize him because I was new in town, but he told me that he was a member at Scioto. His name was Charlie Nicklaus.

Mr. Nicklaus had heard that I was starting a class for junior golfers, and he wondered if his son, Jackie, could join. He said Jackie was only ten but that he liked sports and had quite a bit of athletic ability. I said, "Sure, I'd be glad to have him," and told Mr. Nicklaus when the first session would be held.

That day arrived, and so did the youngsters. It was the first time anyone had ever taught a junior golf class in Columbus and the kids came out of the rafters—about 75 of them. But the first to arrive was young Jack Nicklaus. And in the days and years that followed he almost always was the first to arrive, so that he could be the first in line to be taught.

4

> *"I can remember many times when I was discouraged with my game. I'd come off the course and Jack would be teaching someone else. I'd say to him, 'Jack Grout, will you get finished with that lesson and get over here. I've got to talk to you!' The nice thing about it was that he was always willing to help me. I know he spent more time with me than any other 30 people at Scioto."*—JACK NICKLAUS

My friendship with Jack Nicklaus remains very close after 25 years. He is a perfect example of what it takes to master a game that requires precise physical technique, to be sure, but also dedicated hard work, an intelligent and alert and innovative mind, and great strength of character. Since Jack combines these qualities better, in my opinion, than any other golfer in history, I shall use him frequently throughout this book as a model for you to copy.

In this book I shall teach you the same fundamentals that I taught Jack Nicklaus. They are fundamentals that any person can develop—in fact, *must* develop if he or she is to become a really proficient golfer. I strongly believe that the golf swing is in many ways an *unnatural* maneuver. The person who relies solely on natural athletic talents and normal instincts will sooner or later surely reach a point where improvement stops. To build a golf swing only on natural instinct is to build a swing full of golfing flaws. You can practice hard and long and play frequently, but if your swing is not based on *golfing* fundamentals, you will merely ingrain your mistakes. Unfortunately, because they never learn the fundamentals early enough, that is what 99 percent of golfers presently do.

In this book I will explain not only what you should do to build a solid golf swing, but also why each fundamental is important and how it fits into the swing as a whole. I think it is important that you understand how one thing affects another—what causes what—because, sooner or later, you will be on your own. When that time comes, you will flounder in hit-or-miss fashion unless you understand your own swing and can diagnose your own mistakes. Nicklaus is a fine case in point. I taught him the fundamentals of the game, but there came a time when he had to figure out his own problems and their cures.

"I'd ask questions. Jack Grout would tell me that I should change directions slowly at the top of my backswing. I'd say, 'Why do I have to change directions slowly?' Then he would explain that, if I didn't, my legs wouldn't have time to work in my downswing; my shoulders would take over instead. There's a million things Jack told me to do, but he also always told me why to do them."— JACK NICKLAUS

In this book I will not only tell you how to swing a golf club, and why you should do so in a particular way, but also how to better yourself as a player of the game. There is an art to practicing and taking lessons and learning from watching others. There is an art also to managing your game on the course—selecting the right club, planning your shots, saving strokes when things begin to go sour. And all these factors are just as important to your score as how you actually swing the club.

I will talk about the equipment you need for golf, and the rules you need to know. I'll explain the basic golf etiquette that is essential if you are to become a popular playing companion. I'll tell you how to figure and apply a handicap, since most club competitions involve the giving or receiving of handicap strokes. In short, I will tell you everything you need to know to play and enjoy golf with your friends. Finally, I have included at the end of the book a glossary of golfing terms, because the game has a language of its own and the more fluently you learn to speak it, the more you will enjoy yourself as a golfer.

Throughout the book you will find that Dick Aultman, the former editor of *Golf Digest* magazine who has helped me put my thoughts on paper, has inserted many quotations from Jack Nicklaus. These appear in italicized typeface and are intended to spotlight and stress certain points that I make in the text. Some of them come from Jack's excellent book *Golf My Way*, and some are taken from conversations between us. I am grateful to Jack for letting me voice his views.

While most of the things that are important in learning golf apply to all players, there are certain pieces of advice that apply only to youngsters, or only to adults. Therefore, throughout the book, you will find that in certain sections, all clearly marked, I will be speaking chiefly to young people or their parents, or chiefly to adult newcomers to the game.

Finally, before we proceed, I would like to tell you a few things about golf that perhaps you have not yet had the opportunity to realize. I want you to understand these things so that you can better appreciate what a wonderful and unique game it is, if you have not already found that out for yourself.

Obviously golf is a healthy form of outdoor exercise. If you choose to walk the course, instead of riding in a golf cart, you will stride some four miles or more during every 18-hole round. And you will probably, at first, swing the club with full force some 50 to 100 times.

The more you play, the more you will appreciate the infinite variety of challenges that golf presents. You will find that every shot offers a different set of factors to consider. The wind velocity and direction; the lie of the ball in the grass; the length of the shot; the terrain on which you stand; the softness or hardness of the fairway and the green; trees, sand, water, all these things and many more affect how you perform every time you swing the club.

You will find that golf's challenge is so complete that it makes you forget about any other problems you might have on your mind, thus offering you a healthy escape from day-to-day worries.

You will find that golf, unlike so many other activities in our daily lives, rewards success and penalizes failure *immediately*. You do not need to wait for a teacher or professor to grade your efforts, nor for a corporate profit and loss statement to tell you whether you are succeeding at business. In golf you know as soon as the ball leaves the clubface whether or not you've performed well or poorly.

Golf is a game that brings out both the best and the worst aspects of a person's character. It rewards patience, self-control, and honest self-analysis. It penalizes anger and self-deception. It is a game that pits you alone against the course. And the course doesn't move around to block your shots, or try to knock you out of bounds, or throw you curve balls. It just sits there passively, waiting for you to challenge it—and yourself. In other words, the burden of proof in golf is solely on you, the player, which is one of the chief reasons why it is such a popular and, for many people, a lifelong game.

Also, golf is to some extent a game of luck. You will hit bad shots that finish next to the flagstick, and you will hit good shots that bounce sideways into trouble. In either case, it will be up to you to accept the good breaks and not to let the bad ones throw you off stride.

In some ways golf is a game of strength, but much more it is a game of rhythm, timing, finesse, and mind over matter. It is a game at which men and women who are short in stature and slight of build can, and have, excelled. The ranks of great players, past and present, include far more Davids than Goliaths.

Finally, golf is a game that entices you to try to play better and better, but always leaves room for advancement. The more you play and the better you play, the more you will see areas for improvement and will want to respond to them.

"I have never played golf perfectly, and there is a mighty good chance that neither I nor anyone else ever will. The better I have become, the more I have embarrassed myself by my failure; and the more I have embarrassed myself, the more I have been goaded into trying to develop greater skills. Of this I am presently certain: when failure ceases to embarrass me, and thus to stimulate me to greater efforts, my day will be done and I shall quit playing golf in public."—JACK NICKLAUS

CHAPTER TWO

The Basics of the Game

BEFORE I TELL YOU how to go about striking the ball, let me first explain some basics about the game of golf. Without this knowledge you would be like a baseball player who had learned how to catch, throw, and bat, but didn't know that three strikes were "out" and four balls a "walk." Therefore, in this chapter we'll talk about:

• The golf course itself, so that you will understand the field of battle.

• The rules, so that you won't embarrass yourself by breaking them in front of your friends.

• How to keep score and apply handicap strokes, since they enter into most rounds you play in company.

• Various types of golf competitions you will find yourself involved in sooner or later.

• The game's code of etiquette, so that, even as a novice, you can be a pleasant golfing companion.

• Equipment you will need, and guidelines for purchasing it.

If you are an experienced golfer you may already be aware of much of this information, in which case by all means jump to the next chapter. However, based on my observation of even experienced players over the years, I suspect that some of it will be new to you, so maybe just a quick skim through this chapter would still be worth your while.

THE GOLF COURSE

The golf course is the field of battle on which you will conduct warfare against others, in a friendly but determined fashion. Every golfing field of battle is different from all others, and each varies in many ways from day to day, sometimes from hour to hour, which is one of the great charms of golf.

The more you understand about any particular battlefield, the better your chances for victory. Later on we'll be describing various battle strategies, but for now what I want to point out is that, generally, your chances of beating other players are best when you forget about them and concentrate exclusively on how you, yourself, can best maneuver your own ball around the course.

A round of golf consists of playing 18 "holes" in a prescribed sequence. Thus the war becomes, in effect, 18 different battles. Each hole includes a prepared area, known as a "tee," from which the first shot of each battle is fired. Most holes have at least two tees, one for men and one farther forward for women. Some holes include a third tee farther back, for use in tournaments and for those players who seek an added challenge.

On each tee you will find two markers planted in the ground. You must position your ball—though not yourself—between and within two club-lengths behind these markers. When playing from this area you are allowed to set the ball above the ground by placing it on a special peg, also called a tee.

Each hole also includes a distant area of close-cropped grass known as the "green." A hole 4¼ inches in diameter is cut into each green, and is marked by a flagstick so that you can see where it is located from a distance.

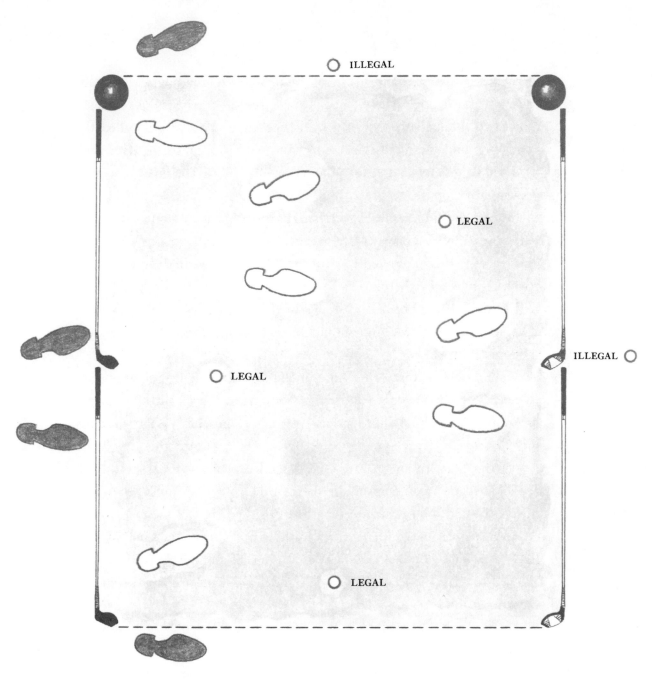

THE TEEING GROUND *is a rectangular area two club-lengths in depth, the front and sides of which are defined by the outside limits of the two markers. For a tee shot to be legal, at least some part of the ball—though not the player himself—must have set within this area. If you violate this rule in match play, your opponent has the right to make you replay your shot, but without your having to take a penalty. In stroke play you must again make your tee shot, counting both that stroke and the original plus any subsequent strokes you might have made before replaying. If you do not replay your tee shot before playing from the next teeing ground, or before leaving the final green of the round, you will be disqualified.*

Between the tee and green of each hole you will find that your route of attack is clearly defined by an area of grass that is regularly mowed to about the height of a well-kept lawn. This area is called the "fairway," and the number of shots you take in your battle with each hole will be greatly reduced if you keep your ball on the fairway as you maneuver it from tee to green.

Most golf holes present certain basic challenges along the way. Adjacent to many fairways and greens you will find "rough," which is grass that has been allowed to grow tall or thick, or both. Shots from rough require special techniques that I will explain later. You will also find yourself behind or under or against trees or bushes at times. As you become a better player you should learn to make shots that overcome such obstacles.

You will find that many holes include "hazards." In golf there are two types of hazards—sand and water. Sand hazards are called "bunkers" or "traps," and also require special playing techniques. Water hazards include streams, rivers, ponds, lakes and the like, even if they might be dry at the time. In any hazard—be it sand or water—because you are not allowed to "test" the surface or texture, your club must not touch the hazard until you actually swing towards the ball.

Many holes have either naturally- or artificially-defined boundaries, beyond which your ball is considered "out of bounds." You are not allowed to play shots from out of bounds, and we'll explain what you must do in this situation a little later.

The length of a golf hole is measured in yards from the middle of the teeing ground to the middle of the green along the line of play intended by the designer of the hole. These distances are printed on the scorecard you can obtain from the pro shop before you play. On the scorecard you will also find that each hole has been assigned a "par," based primarily on its length.

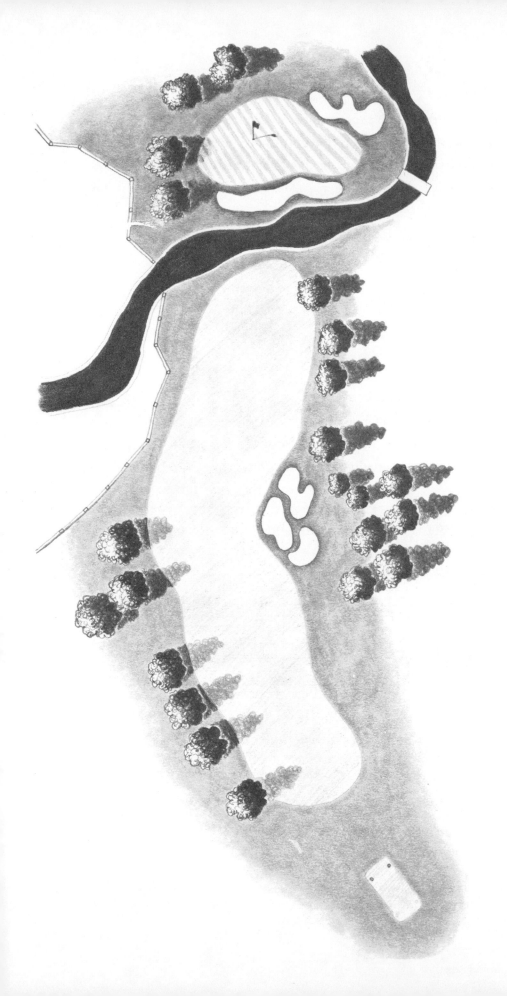

A TYPICAL GOLF HOLE is played from the teeing ground (at left of drawing) to the green (right of drawing). The ideal route of play is usually down the fairway (lighter-shaded area in middle). Areas to avoid include the deeper grass known as "rough" (dark areas along the fairway and around the green), trees, out of bounds (white area to left of fence) and hazards. The latter may be sand (white areas to right of fairway and around the green) and water (black area running in front of the green and around to the right of it).

Par is the score that an expert golfer would be expected to make on the hole if he or she played error-free golf under normal weather conditions, allowing two strokes on the putting green. Here is how the United States Golf Association suggests that par be assigned on holes of various lengths:

LENGTH OF HOLE IN YARDS

Par	Men	Women
3	Up to 250	Up to 210
4	251 to 470	211 to 400
5	471 and over	401 to 575
6	—	576 and over

Most "regulation" golf courses vary in total length between 6,000 and 7,000 yards, and carry a total par of between 70 and 72 for men and 72 and 75 for women. Actually, very few golfers are expert enough to

HOLE	1	2	3	4	5	6	7	8	9	OUT	10	11	12	13	14	15	16	17	18		IN	TOTAL
BLUE	379	368	351	572	150	549	422	176	393	3360	401	548	151	359	394	387	456	254	377		3327	6687
WHITE	368	356	336	529	135	534	402	161	371	3192	362	523	136	346	375	369	426	230	362		3129	6321
HANDICAP	11	9	13	3	17	1	5	15	7		12	2	18	10	14	4	6	16	8			
MEN'S PAR	4	4	4	5	3	5	4	3	4	36	4	5	3	4	4	4	4	3	4		35	71
WOMEN'S PAR	4	4	4	5	3	5	4	3	4	36	4	5	3	4	4	4	5	3	4		36	72
WOMEN'S Y'D'GE	335	344	300	503	121	514	378	148	356	2999	335	490	121	280	341	347	400	185	344		2843	5842
HANDICAP	11	9	13	3	17	1	7	15	5		8	2	18	12	14	4	6	16	10			
DATE				SCORER							ATTESTED											

A TYPICAL SCORECARD—*Names of the players are entered on the left. The numbers of the holes are indicated in the first row across the top. Beneath each hole number are, from top to bottom, yardage from the farthest-back men's tees (blue tees), yardage from the normal men's tees (white tees), the ranking of the hole among all 18 for the awarding of handicap strokes to men, men's par, women's par, yardage from the women's tees, and the order in which strokes are allocated in women's matches. Scores for the first nine holes are totaled and entered in the column headed "out," and for the second nine under the "in" column.*

break or match par regularly, but it represents the target for better players. Until you reach that stage, I suggest that you set a more realistic goal than actual par. Try to average one over par (a "bogey"), or two over (a "double bogey"), or even three over (a "triple bogey"), for the 18 holes, depending on your current stage of development.

THE RULES

• You've just hit a shot into a sand bunker. You look down at the ball and discover that just behind it is a discarded cigarette package. Right in front of the ball lies a large pebble. Both of these objects are likely to make you hit a bad shot. Do the Rules of Golf allow you to lift either the cigarette pack or the pebble? Answer: You can remove the cigarette package, but not the pebble.

• You are playing one of the solid-construction golf balls and it splits in two as you strike it. One part flies into a pond; the other hops up onto the green. Are you allowed to drop a new ball? If so, where? Answer: You *must* replay the shot, but without penalty.

• You've just hit a shot that rebounds off a tree and flies back against your foot. Must you take a penalty for "touching" the ball? Answer: Yes. In "match play" you lose the hole. In "medal" (stroke) play you must add two shots to your score.

These are just three of the thousands of strange things that can and do happen on golf courses every day that require some sort of rules interpretation. Such a wide variety of incidents is to be expected when you consider that golf is a game that, unlike almost any other sport, is played outdoors in a huge, largely undefined, and predominantly natural area—where anything from tree limbs to chipmunks can affect the outcome of your shots.

CHAPTER TWO

The Rules of Golf are established and legislated by the United States Golf Association (USGA) and the Royal and Ancient Golf Club of St. Andrews, Scotland. These governing bodies determine almost everything about golf, from the width of the grooves in your iron clubfaces (no wider than .035 inches), to the length of time you may look for your ball before it is considered lost (five minutes), to whether or not you may borrow an opponent's club during play (you may not).

The rules are so complex that few golfers understand them thoroughly. In fact, I'd guess that nine out of ten golfers inadvertently break at least one rule—and often several—during almost every round they play. Nevertheless, the rules are there for everyone to learn and abide by, and I strongly suggest that you do so for several reasons. First, knowing the rules will save you the embarrassment of breaking them in front of your friends, and add to their respect for you as a person as well as a golfer. Second, knowing the rules will protect you from losing an important competition through breaking one or more of them. (The penalties for rules infractions can actually cause you to be disqualified, though generally they require adding two shots to your score or forfeiting one hole to your opponent.) Third, knowing the rules can actually *save* you strokes in that some of them provide relief when you find your ball, or yourself, in certain difficult situations.

The Rules of Golf are available in a 91-page booklet that you can buy by sending 50 cents to the United States Golf Association, Far Hills, N.J. 07931. Study this booklet and keep it handy in your golf bag.

While the scope of this book does not permit me to detail every rule of golf, there are two basic principles underlying all of the specific rules. Until you have studied the complete set of rules, you will be able to keep any mistakes to a minimum by understanding these principles.

The first of these two basic principles is simply that you play the course as you find it. One reason for this is that golf would be far less challenging if you were allowed, for instance, to stamp down the grass behind your ball, or to have a friend hold back a tree limb that interferes with your swing.

There are some exceptions to this principle that keep golf—though it is a game of luck as well as skill—from becoming unfairly difficult. For instance, you may—and should—repair an indentation in the green made by the landing of your ball or another person's. Except in hazards, you may clear away "loose impediments," these being defined as natural objects not adhering to the ball, such as stones that are not solidly imbedded, leaves, twigs, worms, and the like. You may do the same with "obstructions," even in hazards. An obstruction is anything "artificial," such as a rake, hose, bottle, or cigarette pack.

The second great principle underlying the rules is that once you put your ball into play from the tee, you do not touch it again until you lift it from the hole. In other words, you "play it as it lies." Again, however, there are exceptions, the principle one being that once your ball is on the green you may mark its spot with a coin or other similar object, lift it for cleaning, and then replace it in its original location. Other examples are: unless the ball is in a hazard, you may lift it to see if it's yours; you may lift and replace a damaged ball; and you may lift and drop the ball over your shoulder to gain relief from ground under repair, temporary accumulations of water, and immovable obstructions such as water coolers. However, you cannot drop a ball from a hazard to a point outside it without taking a penalty.

In addition to these exceptions, there will be times when you find that your ball has come to rest in an "unplayable lie," for instance, nestled amid rocks or against a tree trunk. In these circumstances the rules allow you to lift and drop the ball within certain prescribed areas, but require that you take a one-stroke penalty for so doing.

Beyond these exceptions, I again stress that you should not in any way alter the course or move your ball until you understand the rules thoroughly.

It is, for instance, these days an all-too-common practice at many courses to play "winter rules," which allow you to move your ball onto a preferred lie whenever it's in your own fairway. The Rules of Golf do not recognize winter rules and I suggest that, with rare exception, you avoid playing them, for the very good reason that if you get into the habit of shooting only from ideal lies, you'll quickly have trouble hitting from even normal lies when you play with golfers who really stick by the rules. Also, winter rules allow you to shoot deceptively low scores, which result in your being assigned a lower handicap than you deserve. Thus, when you compete against others whose handicaps are realistic, you will not receive as many score-reducing handicap strokes as you need to have a winning chance.

One final point about the rules is that, in golf, you usually have no referee except yourself. Such is the game's code of honor that its history is filled with incidents where players have called penalties on themselves for infractions that no one else was aware had occurred. The player who breaks this code of self-imposed ethics will sooner or later get caught, and will instantly become unpopular with other golfers and, perhaps even more importantly, with himself.

KEEPING SCORE

The number of times you swing at the ball (even if, at first, you miss it completely), plus any penalty strokes, determines your score for any given hole. Your total score for these 18 "battles" determines your score for the round. Thus the object of golf is simply to win the war by taking as few strokes as possible in each battle.

As I've mentioned, there are dozens of rules infractions that require you to add penalty strokes to your score. By far the most common penalties, however, occur when you lose your ball, or hit it out of bounds, or knock it into a water hazard, or find it in an unplayable lie. If you understand what to do in these four situations, you will be able to play golf without fear of embarrassing yourself in front of others.

The lost ball and the out-of-bounds situations are handled identically, the penalty for each being "stroke and distance." In other words, you must add one stroke to your score and replay the shot, thus also losing the distance you had originally gained. Let's say your second shot on a hole became lost or finished out of bounds. You are required to drop a ball over your shoulder at approximately the same spot from which you hit the original shot, add one stroke, and then play what would be, for scoring purposes, your fourth shot.

Returning to the original spot to drop over your shoulder delays play, so, to avoid this problem, if you *think* a shot you've played may be lost or out of bounds, you may immediately drop and play a "provisional ball." If it was your tee shot that appeared headed for trouble, you may play your provisional ball from the wooden peg, instead of dropping it over your shoulder. Naturally, you should remove your provisional ball from play if and when you find that your original shot is not lost or out of bounds.

When your ball finishes in a water hazard and you choose not to try to play it out, you may follow the same procedure and accept the same stroke-and-distance penalty as for a lost ball or ball out of bounds. Alternatively, you may simply drop a ball over your shoulder behind the hazard, anywhere along a line that keeps the original ball's point of entry between where you drop and the hole, and add one penalty stroke to your score. This is usually the preferable procedure in that it will usually save you considerable loss of distance.

COMMON PENALTY SITUATIONS

UNPLAYABLE LIE—*Player may either
(a) replay original shot, count both strokes and
add a penalty stroke, or (b) drop a ball within
two club-lengths of the unplayable lie, but not
nearer the hole, and add one penalty stroke or
(c) drop a ball as far back as desired along a line
that keeps the unplayable lie between the player
and the hole, and add one penalty stroke.*

BALL IN WATER HAZARD—*If player chooses
not to play from the water, he may take a
penalty stroke and (a) drop a ball as far back as
he chooses from the water, keeping the original
shot's point of entry between him and the hole,
or (b) replay the original shot from as near as
possible to the original position. When the water
hazard is considered "lateral" to the hole, the
player has the additional option of taking a
penalty stroke and dropping a ball within two
club-lengths of the hazard, on either side of
it, opposite the original point of entry but not
nearer the hole.*

BALL LOST—*If a player's ball is not found
after five minutes of searching, the player must
replay the original shot, count both strokes and
add one penalty shot.*

BALL OUT OF BOUNDS—*Player must replay
the shot, count both strokes made and add one
penalty shot.*

In the case of an unplayable lie, you have three alternatives: you may replay the shot; or you may drop back anywhere on a line keeping the unplayable position between you and the hole; or you may drop within two club lengths of the unplayable lie, but no closer to the hole. But in each case you must also add one penalty stroke to your score for the hole.

It is also important to know that you are not allowed to play a provisional ball when you suspect that your shot may have gone into a water hazard or an unplayable lie.

HANDICAPPING

"Handicaps" add greatly to the sociability and competitiveness of golf in that they allow players of widely different abilities to play against each other on a more or less equal basis. Thus, if you play golf regularly, you should establish and maintain a handicap. At most clubs a committee or handicap chairman will figure your handicap for you periodically. If this service is not available, ask your club pro how you can obtain an official handicap.

Briefly, your handicap is based on the difference between the United States Golf Association difficulty "ratings" (not the pars) of the courses where you've played your last 20 rounds and the scores you've shot. If you take the ten lowest of these differences and find their average, your handicap will be 85 percent of that figure (96 percent as of January 1, 1976).

Obviously, the better you play, the lower your handicap becomes. Thus if you post all your scores, good or bad—as you should do—your handicap becomes a very accurate reflection of your current playing ability. Moreover, when you enter a handicap competition, or even when you play a friendly game for stakes or mere pride, your handicap will determine how many strokes you must give to, or receive from, your rivals.

If you compete with handicap at match play, in which the victor is the golfer winning the most holes, the difference between your handicap and your opponent's will determine the number of holes on which you must give, or will receive, a stroke reduction. In other words, if your handicap is, say, 20 and your opponent's 12—a difference of eight—you will receive a one-stroke reduction on each of the eight lowest ranked "stroke holes."

The stroke hole ranking of each hole is given on the scorecard and is based primarily on its scoring difficulty; the hole on which players normally require the most strokes being ranked number one. Thus, if your handicap were three strokes higher than your opponent's, you would receive a one-shot reduction on the three holes where you were most likely to shoot your highest scores, which would be shown on the scorecard as stroke holes one, two, and three.

GOLF EVENTS

Whatever your reason for learning to play golf, be it merely to get outdoors and have fun or someday to win the U.S. Open, you will find your enjoyment and appreciation of the game greatly increased if you compete against others whenever possible. Even if the prize is only a small trophy or a 50-cent side bet, competition will give you added reason to meet the challenges inherent in the game and to improve your skill at it.

I've pointed out how handicaps allow even a newcomer to compete against the club champion in certain tournaments. Other events do not involve handicaps and thus do not involve the giving or taking of strokes, but are determined by gross score. However, even in these events, golfers are usually grouped with players of similar ability to ensure that everyone has a good chance to win a prize. In these events you are assigned to a group, either on the basis of your handicap or on the score you shoot in one or more qualifying rounds.

I've mentioned that stroke play tournaments are those based on total score for the round or rounds (most professional tournaments consist of four rounds at stroke play). Match play involves trying to win more holes than you lose to your opponent. If, for instance, you win four holes and your opponent wins only three, you are a "one up" winner. The match need not go the full distance. It would end, for instance, if you or your opponent were four holes "up" with only three holes left in the round.

Sometimes, in both stroke and match play, you will find yourself tied with an opponent after all holes have been completed. Generally such a tie will be broken by playing extra holes at "sudden death," until you or your opponent wins a hole. In very serious competition, however, the tournament committee will often require an 18-hole playoff. In both cases in handicap tournaments, the "stroke holes" remain the same as those originally allotted.

Not only will you find yourself playing both match play and stroke play, with or without handicaps, but also you will play in "four-ball" events (often erroneously called "foursomes" in the United States. A foursome is actually a contest between teams of two players hitting all shots alternately). Here you compete with a partner against other two-man teams, with everyone playing his own ball but only the better score of each team counting on each hole. If the competition is played with handicaps, it is the lowest "net" ball of each team that counts. The "best-ball" format is by far the most common in the United States whenever four people get together for a round of golf, and the winner is usually determined by match play—holes won and lost—rather than total strokes played for the round.

BETTING

Within these basic types of competition, you will generally find yourself involved in various side games which usually involve some sort of betting. If the stakes aren't too high, these games and bets add spice and fun to the round.

Usually the amount of money involved is minimal, representing more a token of victory than a means to supplement one's income, and I strongly advise against allowing yourself to become involved in betting beyond your means, or to the point where winning or losing might create hard feelings.

The most common golf betting game is the "nassau" match. Here, individuals or teams play the first nine holes for a given prize, the second nine for a similar prize, and the overall 18 holes for the same or a slightly higher amount. The appeal of this type of bet is that it gives incentive to do well on the second nine if you may have done poorly on the first. Often, within the nassau match, you also find the element of "press" betting, whereby the player or team that is losing may "press" by asking that an additional prize—usually equal to the original amount—be awarded to the winner of the remaining holes of the nine being played.

Side betting may also involve a prize for "greenies"—for putting one's tee shot on the green and closer to the hole than that of any of the other players. "Syndicates" or "skins" or "scats" are prizes for the player whose score on a hole is lower than that of any of his fellow competitors. Frequently it will also be agreed that prizes be awarded for "birdies," a score of one under par on any hole.

Thus, within a typical group of four golfers playing together, two might be playing the other pair a nassau match, with presses allowed, plus each individual playing each of the others a nassau match, also including presses, with extra prizes awarded for any birdies and greenies. Obviously, such a battle keeps everyone interested and competitive and creates a great deal of friendly banter, both during and after the round.

There are literally dozens of other golf events and betting forms too numerous to mention here. However, if you understand these basic types you will have little or no trouble understanding the others.

ETIQUETTE

Traditionally, golf is a gentleman's game, which means that failure to observe certain courtesies will definitely offend most of those you play with and also, at times, all others on the course. However, by observing the simple rules of etiquette that follow, you can be assured that you will be an acceptable golfing companion, regardless of your current playing ability.

• Have your club in hand and be ready to play the shot immediately when it is your "honor" or turn. Honor on the tee is determined by scores on the previous hole. The golfer with the lowest score tees off first, the next lowest second, and so on. In the case of ties between two or more players, refer back to the last hole on which the tie was broken. In team matches the side that last won a hole has the honor. Following tee shots, it is always the player whose ball is farthest from the hole who plays first.

• Do not delay another golfer from playing when it is his or her honor. Save your conversation for when you are walking down the fairway or to the next tee.

- If you are playing slowly or looking for a lost ball, signal any group waiting behind you to "play through."
- Do not talk or even move while others are swinging or preparing to swing.
- Do not stand in the range of vision of anyone who is preparing to play.
- Do not let your shadow fall into another player's field of vision while he or she is swinging.
- Replace any turf (divot) you dislodge in making a shot and press it down gently with your foot.
- Never pull or drive your cart or golf car across a green or through a sand bunker.
- Carefully smooth out any marks you make in sand bunkers.
- Repair ball marks made by the landing of your shots and others' on the greens.
- Before putting, set your bag or park your golf car or cart on the side of the green nearest the next tee, to avoid delay between holes.
- On the green, do not step on the probable path of another golfer's putt.
- Leave the putting green as soon as your group has finished. Mark your scorecard on the next tee while others shoot.
- Avoid detailed and boring post-round narratives about how you played various shots.
- Control your temper at all times.

EQUIPMENT

The equipment you choose for golf depends primarily on two things: how much you can afford to pay, and how well you hope to play. It is possible to enjoy the game using merely a handful of cheap store-bought or secondhand clubs, a dozen or so cheap "discount store" balls, a pair of inexpensive golf shoes (or even sneakers), a light canvas bag, and a 25-cent pack of tees. I must warn you, however, that in the long run you will never play up to your full golfing potential with such equipment.

On the other hand, you can spend as much as $2,000 for a set of graphite-shafted clubs, put them in a $200 leather bag, fill the bag with everything from a $50 rain suit to insect repellent, don a $60 pair of golf shoes and $60 worth of golf slacks and shirt, and use a new top-quality ball every third hole.

Somewhere in between these two extremes lies a logical investment that fits your golfing needs and your wallet. (Even Jack Nicklaus does not use anywhere near so costly a set of clubs as I've mentioned above, although he does carry two identical sets to tournaments in case one is lost, damaged or stolen.) In the end, you will have to decide for yourself what purchases you should make, but I'd be happy here to try to help you to make a sound decision.

Your most important—and probably most expensive—purchase will be a set of clubs. The rules allow you to carry no more than 14 clubs, and one of these will most certainly be a putter, for rolling the ball on the shorter grass of the greens. The rest of your set will consist of "woods," so called because their heads are mostly wooden, and "irons," which have metal heads.

Today, most golfers carry three or four woods and nine or ten irons, plus a putter. Most sets of woods include a No. 1 wood (known as the "driver"), a 3 wood, a 4 wood, and a 5 wood. You can include a 2 wood but, because of the 14-club limit, most people find it serves relatively little purpose. A typical set of irons will include a 2 iron, 3 iron, 4 iron, 5 iron, 6 iron, 7 iron, 8 iron, 9 iron and a fairway (pitching) wedge and a sand wedge. Since most golfers handle bunker shots much better with a sand wedge than with a pitching wedge or a 9 iron, they include it in their set and still remain within the 14-club limit by dropping either the 2 iron or the 4 wood or 5 wood (but not both).

Each wood and iron club is built to hit shots of different distances and heights. The factors that produce these differences are the overall length of the club and its "loft." Loft is the degree at which the clubface slants backward when the sole of the club is set squarely on the ground.

All things being equal, the more loft you have on the face of the club, the more it will hit shots upward as opposed to forward. This is true not only because of the loft itself, but also because additional loft applies additional backspin to the ball, and additional backspin decreases distance by increasing height. Also, the greater the loft the club carries, the less forward momentum it can apply to the ball.

The distance of a shot is also affected by the overall length of the club. The longer the club, the bigger the arc on which the clubhead travels during the swing, and the bigger the arc, the greater the potential clubhead speed during impact with the ball. The greater the clubhead speed at impact, the further the ball will go if squarely struck.

Woods and irons are numbered so that you can tell at a glance which is which. The lower the number on the club, the less its loft and the greater its length. Thus, among the woods, the No. 1 wood, or "driver," is the longest-shafted and least lofted, and theoretically at least will hit shots farther than will a 3 wood, which in turn will hit longer shots than a 4 wood.

The same holds true for the irons. A 2 iron, with its lesser loft and longer shaft, will hit shots farther than will a 3 iron. Three-iron shots generally go farther than 4-iron shots, and so on, all the way up to the shortest and most-lofted club, the sand wedge, which hits shots a shorter distance in relationship to height than any other iron or wood.

In a later chapter I will go into detail about which clubs to use, and how to use them, for different types of shots. Now, however, the thing that I want to make very clear is that your clubs directly determine the manner in which you swing, in that, if they do not fit you properly, they will force you to a greater or lesser degree to swing incorrectly. Also, if your clubs do not match one another in certain ways, they will force you into the complicated matter of developing a slightly different swing for each differing club in the set.

For these reasons, I strongly suggest that you take some lessons from a golf pro before buying your clubs. The pro will not only improve your swing tremendously, but will thereafter fit you with clubs that match your new and improved swing pattern. I think it makes good sense that, if you are going to spend $400–$500 for a full set of high-quality clubs that will last you for several years, you should also invest another $75–$100 in lessons so that you will swing them well, and so that they will match your swing.

It is possible to buy a full set of clubs from a retail store for less than half the price you would pay for a set from a golf pro. Consider, however, that the store-bought clubs probably will not:

• Incorporate the very latest technological developments in club design.

• Measure up in overall quality to the pro's set.

• Match each other within the set.

• Fit your particular swing needs.

• Be tradeable for a new set when the time comes for a change.

Regarding the fourth point, I think you should understand some of the various ways that clubs can be fitted to your swing pattern if purchased through a golf pro.

The most important consideration in fitting clubs is the type of shaft selected. Shafts come in various degrees of flex, or "whippiness." Generally, the whippier the shaft, the greater your ability to "feel" the clubhead. Thus, given that you strike the ball solidly, a whippier shaft might give you slightly more distance. However, the downside to this possibility is that whippy shafts require a more precise timing of the delivery of the clubhead to the ball. This is especially true if you happen to have a relatively fast swing, in that the faster you swing, the more the whippier clubshaft will bend and twist. Therefore I generally recommend relatively stiff shafts for most men and for stronger women golfers. Weaker men and most women, I find, play better with shafts of normal flex.

Another factor is the length of the shafts. While clubs within any set vary in length to produce different types of shots, it is possible to buy full sets—or individual clubs within a set—that are longer or shorter than average. Longer clubs can produce longer shots because they allow a longer and wider swing arc, but, again, the longer the club the more difficult it is to control.

Often a golfer who is exceptionally tall or short may need clubs that are longer or shorter than average. However, factors more crucial than your height in determining club length are the length of your arms, the distance you stand from the ball, your posture at the ball, and the actual pattern of your swing. For example, it is conceivable that a 6′ 6″ golfer with very long arms might need shorter clubs than a person of average height. If the taller person bought longer clubs, he might stand too far from the ball which, in turn, would make him swing incorrectly.

Equally important as length is the "lie" of your clubs. A club's lie is the angle formed by its head and shaft where they join. This angle is correct for you when the bottom of the club sets flat on the ground when you correctly set up to the ball in your "address position."

If you set up correctly and the outer part of the clubhead—its "toe"—doesn't rest on the ground, your club's lie is too "upright." In that case, unless you make some adjustment during your swing or stand too close to the ball, your club's "heel" will dig into the turf and cause your club-

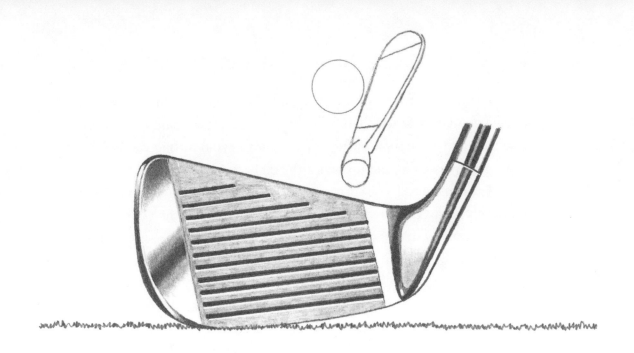

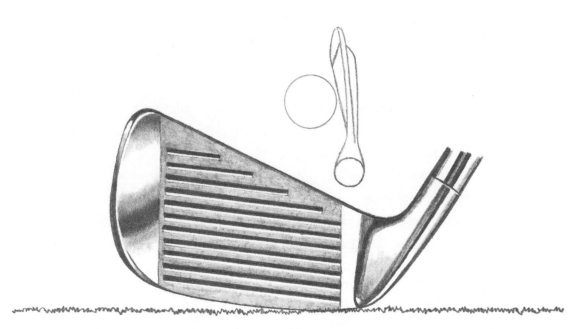

HOW DOES YOUR GOLF CLUB "LIE"?—*The "lie" of a golf club is the angle formed by the clubshaft and the bottom of the clubhead. If the lie of your club is correct, the bottom of the clubhead will rest flat on the ground when you assume a correct address position preparatory to swinging. If your clubhead rests on its outer portion at address (top drawing), its lie is too "flat." The toe of the clubhead will tend to cut into the turf during impact and turn the clubface "open", to the right of target. If your clubhead rests on its inner portion at proper address position (lower drawing), the club's lie is too "upright." The heel of the club will tend to cut into the ground during impact and slow down. Then the clubface "closes" and hits the ball left of target.*

face to turn left of target during impact. The opposite clubface twisting occurs if your lie is too "flat," forcing you to either stand too far from the ball or to make some swing adjustment to avoid hitting the ball right of target by catching the turf with the club's toe.

The diameter of your grips determines how you will hold your club. Generally, grips that are too thick will make you hold the club in a way that will cause you to "slice" shots to the right if you are a righthander. Conversely, grips that are too thin may cause shots to "hook" to the left.

The weighting of your clubs is yet another factor that can influence your degree of success or failure. Clubs that are too heavy may cause you to lose clubhead speed, and thus distance, especially during the latter stages of a round when you might be tiring. Clubs that are too light for you, especially in their heads, may cause a loss of "feel," and thereby a reduced sense of "rhythm" and "timing." The trend today is toward lighter clubshafts and, thus, to lighter overall club weight. But clubs that are *too* light can cause you to swing too fast at the wrong part of your swing.

By now it should be apparent why I suggest that you buy clubs that have been tailored to your physique and your swing pattern, rather than to a national average. With rare exception, only a golf pro can perform such tailoring or obtain clubs with your personal specifications custom-built into them.

Most manufacturers make various types of balls, even though they may all look alike, and the type you use is largely a matter of personal taste. There are golf balls made entirely of solid materials that do not cut; balls made of tightly wound rubber and covered with cut-resistant material; tightly wound balls with thin covers that do cut easily, and so on. Inexperienced players who mishit many shots generallly prefer the non-cuttable or cut-resistant balls, while most better players prefer the "feel" and flight characteristics of thin-covered, wound-rubber balls.

Balls are graded by their "compression." A 70 compression ball will "flatten" to a greater extent on the clubface during impact than will an 80 compression ball, which will, in turn, be softer than a 90 or 100 compression ball.

Many golfers prefer a lower compression ball because it feels "softer" when struck. As a rule, however, the higher the ball's compression, the farther it will go, even though it will not compress so readily. I suggest that you use a high-compression ball for maximum distance, but not so high that it feels rock hard when struck. Even many touring professionals prefer balls of slightly less than top compression, either because their extra flattening allows the application of more backspin or sidespin, or simply because they "feel" better at impact.

Any golf professional will advise you about which brands of balls are high or low compression. Whichever you select, however, I suggest that you always buy top quality, because the difference in price between the best, about $1.35 each, and a 75-cent cheapy is minimal when compared to your overall golfing expenses, but the difference in terms of distance and general playability is considerable.

Golf shoes and gloves are vital if you are to play up to your full potential. You need the spikes for footwork and balance as you swing, and the glove for maximum control over the club. Without both you cannot swing as freely and fully as you might.

Shoes vary in cost from about $20 to $60, so economics is a factor in their selection. Generally, however, you will find that the more you pay, the longer the shoes will last and the more comfort they will provide. Comfort and support of the feet are vital factors in golf because it is difficult to play well when you are walking several miles on sore soles and tired legs. I also strongly suggest that you buy shoes that are waterproof.

Gloves are generally worn only on the righthander's left hand and the lefthander's right hand. Buy the most expensive glove you can find in your pro shop. It will cost only two or three dollars more than the cheapest, and it will be thinner, more durable and less susceptible to stretching. Ask the golf shop attendant to help you find one that fits properly—which means very snugly.

Golf bags come in myriad types, sizes, colors, and qualities. I suggest you consider these points before buying:

• A big, durable bag lasts longer, protects clubs better, and holds more miscellaneous equipment—even shoes and laundry—when you travel to play golf.

• A smaller, lighter bag costs less and saves you or your caddie wear and tear.

Many avid golfers buy both the first type—as a long-term investment, and for travel, tournament play and storing extra clothing when wet or cold weather threatens—and the second, lighter bag for everyday play in nice weather. I suggest, however, that you avoid bags that are so cheaply made that they jam your clubs together, allow rain or dew to soak through, or lack sufficient support and balance for easy carrying.

In addition to the above, you will need tees, a golf umbrella, a windbreaker jacket, a box of stretchable band-aids for sore hands and fingers, and possibly suntan lotion and a golf hat. Personally, I feel a hat is a must to protect you from sunstroke on hot days and to ease the sun's glare, which can make judging distance extremely difficult. If you plan to play a lot of golf and to enter tournaments, you will find a rain suit invaluable for those wet and cold days when you must forge ahead.

ADVICE FOR JUNIORS

If you are under 5′ 4″ tall, or if you are not as strong as a normal 15-year-old, standard adult clubs will probably be too long or too heavy for you to swing easily, leading to bad playing habits. Instead, go for a full set of junior-sized clubs.

If you are just starting golf, you might ask your father or your club professional to cut down a secondhand set of clubs to fit your size. If you find that you like golf, and if you can afford new junior clubs, you should buy a set of these when you get to be 11 or 12 years old. If you cannot afford a full set of 14 clubs, get one that includes one or two woods, about four irons, and a putter. That set may last you until you are big and strong—and wealthy—enough to buy a full set of adult clubs.

Since you will probably be carrying your own bag, don't get one that is too heavy. I do suggest that you use golf shoes and a golf glove, but if your feet are growing rapidly you probably should not buy expensive shoes.

Finally, be sure you understand all the rules of etiquette in this chapter. On a golf course you should always act like an adult—just as if you were Jack Nicklaus.

CHAPTER THREE

Concepts of the Swing

I'VE BEEN TOLD that if you take an infant child and drop it into a swimming pool, it will somehow manage to paddle around without drowning. This may be true, but it's a theory I would hate to test.

Most people jump into golf the same way. They go to the course or a practice range, start hitting shots, and hope for the best. They have little or no real understanding about what they are trying to do or about how to do it. I guess most such golfers do manage to keep afloat, but barely. They paddle around golf courses the rest of their lives, struggling to keep their heads above water. At some point many finally seek professional help, but all too often they've been grooving a bad swing for so long that it becomes extremely difficult for them to develop a new, good swing pattern.

Let me right away tell you an infrequently acknowledged truth about golf. It is a highly complex maneuver in which every bone, muscle and fiber in your body has a certain function to perform in a certain way at a certain time. No teacher could possibly explain all those functions, and no person could possibly execute them consciously. He would have to be a human computer.

"Through slow-motion movies, high-speed stop-action cameras, and other new devices, we have been able to isolate and examine major swing moves and to understand more and more clearly how they influence the shot that ensues. However, there is still a lot about the swing that we don't know and probably never will, since hitting correct golf shots can never be a purely scientific proposition."—JACK NICKLAUS

Now, before you turn to tennis, I want to quickly add that it *is* possible to teach and learn certain *fundamentals* of the golf swing. Once you more or less master these fundamentals, it does become possible repeatedly to bring your bones and muscles into play in more or less the right way at more or less the right time. You won't put it all together perfectly on every shot. Even Jack Nicklaus mishits far more shots, to some degree, than he strikes 100 percent "pure." But, once you learn the fundamentals, you *will* excel as a golfer for as long as you maintain your desire and willingness to play and practice.

"If there is one thing I have learned during my years as a professional, it is that the only constant thing about golf is its inconstancy. As an amateur there

were times when I believed that if only I didn't have to clean up my room, or get an education, or earn a living, I would be able to hone my game to a point of absolute perfection and then hold it there permanently. . . . Perfect repetition. Flawless automation. This was my dream. All I needed was sufficient time to work at my game.

"I was kidding myself. When I turned professional, suddenly I had all the time and opportunity I needed. And I discovered, fast, that my dream was just that: a dream. No matter how much work I did, one week I would have it and the next I couldn't hit my hat."—JACK NICKLAUS

I could explain golf's fundamentals as I see them to you now, but first I want to prepare you for learning them by explaining some overall concepts about hitting a golf ball. Once you understand these concepts, it will be much simpler for you to understand and apply the fundamentals contained in the next chapter.

First, you should understand exactly what happens on a good golf shot. Imagine, if you will, that your ball is sitting on the grass and that your target is the distant hole in the green as marked by the flagstick. Let's assume that you want to strike the ball so that it flies on a straight line to your target with just enough length to finish in the hole.

Now, imagine a line running from the flagstick back to your ball and a few feet beyond. This is called your "target line." When you stand up to hit this shot, the area on *your* side of this target line is called "inside the line." The area on the other side is called "outside the line."

INSIDE

OUT

THE ROUTE OF THE GOLF SWING—*The imaginary line from the target to the ball and beyond is the "target line." When playing for a straight shot, the area on your side of this line is called "inside the line." The area on the far side is "outside the line." In the proper golf swing, the clubhead moves inside the line and up during the backswing. It moves from inside to ALONG the line during the downswing, and then back to the inside and up on the follow-through. The overall forward swing is thus down and up, and from the inside to ALONG to inside the line as well. Most golfers make the mistake of swinging the clubhead ACROSS the line, from outside to inside, through impact.*

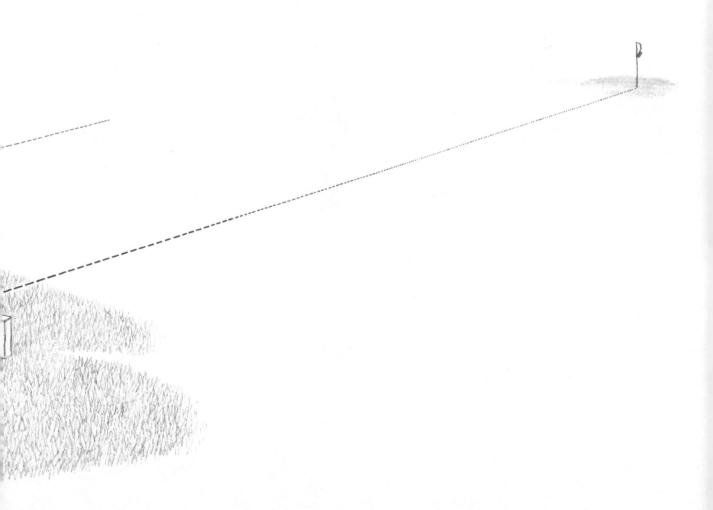

Chapter Three

The first requirement for a good golf shot is that your club's head be moving momentarily along your target line when it impacts the ball. Your shot cannot fly straight towards your target if your clubhead is moving *across* this line in any direction at impact.

For as long as you play golf remember this: your shot will always *start out* in the direction your clubhead was moving during impact. If your clubhead was cutting across from outside the line to inside the line, the ball will start out to the left of target if you are a righthanded golfer. If the clubhead was cutting from inside to outside the line, the ball must at least start out to the right of target. (Henceforth, I will assume that you play golf righthanded. If you are a southpaw, merely assume whenever I say "right" that I mean "left" for you.)

At this point you may wonder what is so difficult about simply swinging the clubhead down your chosen line. The complication is that

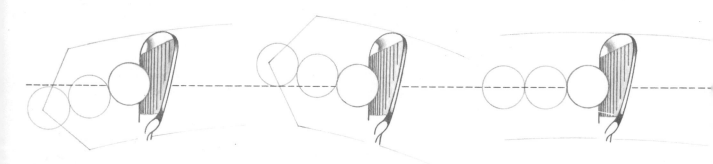

THE INITIAL DIRECTION *in which a golf shot takes off is determined primarily by the path on which the clubhead is moving when it releases the ball. Here we see three impact situations with the clubface alignment identical in each; all are facing down the line. However, each is moving in a different direction. Thus each shot will start its flight in a different direction. While clubhead path determines a shot's early flight direction, sidespin may make it curve left or right thereafter. Wise golfers learn to check their shots' direction of takeoff to discover the path on which they are swinging the clubhead.*

you are standing to one side of the ball as you swing, which means that you must swing the club to a greater or lesser degree *around* yourself. Thus the clubhead must move *inside* the target line during your backswing, and must also return from inside that line if it is to travel along that line at impact. Once the clubhead moves outside the line on your downswing, it is mechanically *impossible* for it to travel *along* it at impact. And understand also that the proper clubhead path is from inside, to along, to back *inside* the target line on your forward swing. In other words, on normal shots the clubhead should never cross the target line, either before or during or after impact.

In addition to the on-line clubhead path, there is a second requirement for the perfectly straight shot you've planned to play. At impact your clubhead must be facing in exactly the same direction as it is moving. In short, it must be at a 90° angle (or "square") to your target line.

Obviously, if your clubhead is moving down the line but your clubface is not square to its path of movement, you must impact the ball with a glancing blow. If the clubface "looks" to the right of its path of movement, it will impart sidespin that will make the ball curve ("slice") to the right. If it faces left of its path of movement during impact, it will apply sidespin in the opposite direction so that the ball will "hook" to the left.

Thus, in order to strike a shot solidly and without sidespin, the clubface must be looking in the same direction as the clubhead is moving at impact. And, for the shot to fly toward the target, the clubhead must be moving along the target line. Thus the clubface must be "square" to the target line.

At this point you might ask, "Why not keep the clubface looking at the target throughout the swing?" Again because you are standing alongside the target line, this is almost an anatomical impossibility. At best, trying to keep the clubface on target throughout a full swing would require a tremendous amount of complicated twisting of the club with your hands, wrists, and arms.

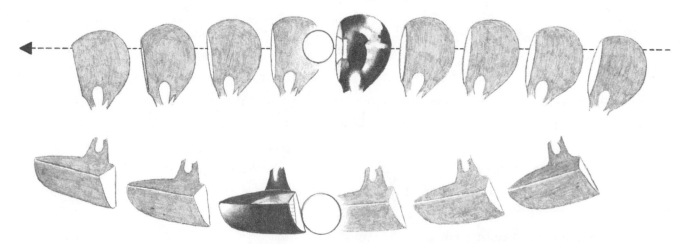

PERFECT IMPACT *can occur only when the clubhead is moving along the line and with its face looking straight down that line (top row of drawings), and when the clubhead is more or less at ball level (second row of drawings). Note that the clubhead moves onto the target line along a path that is slightly from inside the line (top row), and that it gradually descends to ball level (second row).*

IMPERFECT IMPACT—*When the clubhead path is incorrectly across the line from outside to inside (lower left-hand drawing), the angle of descent automatically becomes too steep. The force of the blow is not only to the left of target but also too much downward instead of forward. When the path is too far from the inside (lower right-hand drawing) the angle of attack becomes too shallow. The force of the blow is toward the right of target and, frequently, upward, because the clubhead has touched down well behind the ball.*

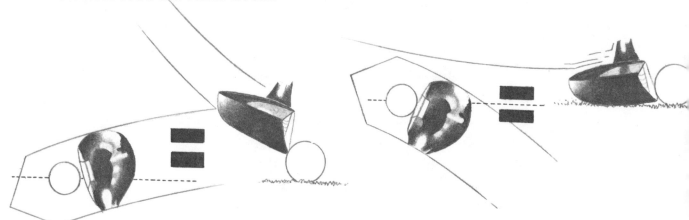

Much more simple and practical is to let the clubface turn naturally as a normal result of your body's turning and your arms' swinging the club. This does not mean, however—as we shall see later—*twisting* the clubface independently with your hands and wrists.

A third requirement for a good shot is that your clubhead be moving more or less at ball level on impact.

Now, it may seem overly simple for me to point out that during the golf swing the clubhead swings up and down and up again, as well as around your body, and it may seem equally obvious that at the bottom of this arc the clubhead should be at ball level. What may not be obvious, however, is that the clubhead's "angle of attack" toward the ball should not be too steep or too shallow. If this angle of attack is too steep—too sharply downward—the force of your shot will be predominantly downward rather than forward, and the ball will not travel as far as it should. Conversely, if your angle of attack is too shallow, you run a big risk of either stubbing the club into the ground behind the ball or catching the ball on your upswing, after your clubhead has already passed the bottom of its arc.

What may also be news to you—even if you are already an experienced golfer—is that your clubhead path directly affects your angle of attack. It does so as follows.

In returning the clubhead to the ball on the downswing, the more from *inside* the target line the clubhead is moving, the *shallower* your angle of attack will be. Conversely, the more your clubhead moves back to the ball from *outside* the line, the *steeper* will be its angle of approach to the ball. It is important for you to understand this relationship of clubhead path to angle of attack in order to understand some of the swing fundamentals we shall examine later.

By now these things should be clear to you:

• The proper golf swing is from inside, to along, to inside the target line.

• The golf swing is up, down, and up again.

• The clubface gradually turns away from the target in a clockwise motion as your body turns away and your arms swing the club around and up on your backswing.

• To make a straight and solid shot, the clubhead, during impact, must be moving along the target line, must be facing "square" to that path of movement, and must be at ball level.

• Your angle of attack must not be too steep or too shallow.

If all these ingredients are correct, your shot will be solidly struck, and your ball will fly straight toward your target. However, one other ingredient is necessary for your shot to succeed: the ball must travel the correct *distance*.

Obviously, your shot's length will be determined at least in part by how squarely your clubface contacts the ball. This is true in any sport where you strike a ball with some other implement—baseball and tennis, for example. If you hit the baseball near the handle of the bat, or the tennis ball near the edge of the racket, the contact will sting or jar your hands and the ball may not get out of the infield, or over the net. So it is in golf; if you catch the ball on the toe or heel of your clubhead, or if your clubface cuts across the ball instead of swinging directly into it, the ball will not travel as far as it would if struck solidly.

While square contact is needed to strike a golf ball a goodly distance, one other factor also determines how far it will travel. That factor is clubhead speed at impact. And here the rule is simple: given solid contact, the faster your clubhead moves into the ball, the further the shot will go with any given club.

How do we achieve maximum clubhead speed? It is important that you understand very clearly the answer to this question, and that you learn to apply it to your swing. Most golfers either don't know how to generate clubhead speed, or, if they do, they go about it the wrong way, which is why they never hit the ball as far as they could.

Clubhead speed comes from building as much potential energy as you can during your *backswing*, and then releasing it *fully* and *at the right time* in your *forward swing*. Please reread that sentence several times, because it contains certain hidden secrets that will help to make you an accomplished golfer.

Within this key statement is the hidden secret that one purpose of the backswing is to *build up* energy, not to waste it. Swinging back too fast wastes energy and may cause you to lose control of the club. A slower, wider backswing, with a full turning of your body, is more likely to build energy. Remember that we are trying to drive the ball *forward*.

"I believe you cannot start the golf club back too slowly, provided you swing it back rather than take it away from the ball. . . . On every shot I endeavor to swing the club into motion very deliberately, very positively, only just fast enough to avoid jerkiness. . . . The harder I want to swing, the slower I try to start back."—JACK NICKLAUS

A second purpose of the backswing is to set your golf club in proper position for starting your forward swing. Ideally, you should set the club at the top of your backswing so that its shaft *parallels* your target line. Imagine that your golf club were, say, 200 yards long. At the top of your swing this club would never point away from your target line, nor would it cut across it. It would run parallel to it, like two railroad tracks.

What setting the club parallel to your target line does is put it: (1)

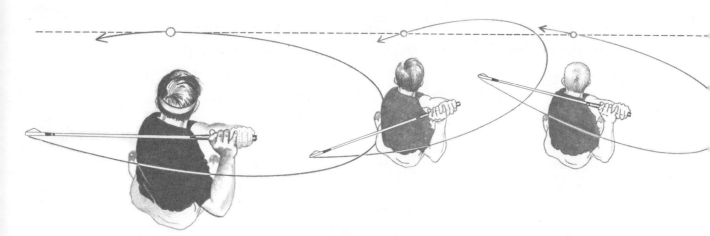

A PURPOSE OF THE BACKSWING *is to set the club into a position from which it will "find" the proper downswing path without the player's having to guide or steer it back to the ball. Setting the clubshaft parallel to the intended line of the shot (left-hand figure) generally allows for an uninhibited, yet accurate, downswing. Pointing the club too far to the left (middle figure) or to the right (right-hand figure) usually results in an across-the-line clubhead path—from outside-in or inside-out respectively—during impact.*

in suitable position to return to the ball *along the target line and at a proper angle of attack,* and (2) in the ideal position for you to swing it *freely* down and forward. Given this positioning at the top, you will never need to guide or manipulate the club into the ball in order to make solid contact. Proper setting on the backswing allows a full, free release of energy on the forward swing.

Our key statement on clubhead speed also contains the hidden secret that you must release your pent-up energy *fully* at the *proper time* in your forward swing.

In the next chapter I will go into more detail about how to do that. For now, what I want you basically to understand is that achieving top clubhead speed during impact is never simply a matter of brute strength —indeed, trying to "muscle" the ball creates tension that actually *reduces* clubhead speed.

Proper *timing* is what produces a *gradual* build-up of clubhead speed during the downswing and a full *release* of it into the ball. Too much effort too early in your downswing can cause you to waste your energy too soon, and to throw your club into a position from which it is impossible to make solid contact.

ADVICE TO JUNIORS

At this point in your golfing life, I think you should be trying to hit your drives as far as you possibly can. This will stretch your muscles and get you into the habit of using all your power.

"Like Arnold Palmer, who's still no patsy off the tee, I was taught to hit the ball hard from the day I first picked up a golf club. Jack Grout encouraged me to spend a lot of my practice time swinging all-out with scant regard to where the ball went. . . . Believe me, whatever arguments those short knockers may throw at you, distance is a huge asset in golf. I certainly encourage my own boys to swing hard through the ball and, thankfully, they seem to have my appetite for it."—JACK NICKLAUS

You may not always hit the ball as solidly or as straight as you would like, but you can always develop better control as you get older.

Another concept you should understand before we get into specific swing fundamentals is what makes a golf ball go up, or not go up; and what makes it fly straight, or curve sideways. In short, you should know about *spin*.

Back in golf's early days, when the solid gutta-percha balls first began to replace the feather-filled, leather-cased balls, their surfaces were originally made smooth. However, it didn't take players long to discover that their shots flew higher and further after this smooth surface had been chewed up a bit by mishitting. Today, of course, there are dimples in the ball to help you to apply spin. As the ball flies through the air, it will go up or down or sideways according, in large part, to the direction and the amount that it is spinning.

For a golf shot to fly through the air, the ball *must* backspin to some degree. This spin creates a "cushion" of air under the ball that helps to keep it aloft. Thus backspin, along with clubhead speed and clubface loft, determines how high and far a ball will carry. A ball that doesn't carry backspin has only the force of the blow and the loft of the club to put it into the air, and it will drop to earth quickly. A ball that carries over-spin or topspin will actually nosedive.

Sidespin causes shots to curve from left to right or right to left in flight. You'll find that it is easier to curve shots with your less-lofted clubs—the woods and longer irons—than with your highly-lofted shorter irons, in that the greater loft of the shorter irons generally produces more backspin, and the greater the backspin the more it tends to offset the affect of any sidespin.

There are four principles to remember about spin in golf:

1. The ball will spin *only* when struck with a glancing blow.

2. To produce a glancing blow, the clubface must be *looking* in a different direction than the clubhead is *moving* as the ball is struck.

3. Sidespin will cause the ball to curve in the direction the clubface was looking, and away from the direction the clubhead was moving, on impact.

4. The greater the *difference* between where the clubhead was facing and where it was moving on impact, the greater the amount of spin applied to the ball—and the greater its curve in relation to distance traveled.

I know this is a lot to digest all at once, so I will give you some examples to explain these important principles.

Example 1: At impact the clubhead is moving *parallel* to the ground at *ball level;* the clubhead is moving *down* the target line; the clubface is *square* to this path of movement.

At first glance, it might seem that these conditions would *not* cause a glancing blow and therefore, according to principle 1, would *not* produce spin. What you must remember is that every club in your bag, except perhaps your putter, carries some degree of clubface loft—in other words, the face looks upward to some extent.

Because of this loft, in this example the clubface is looking *upward* while the clubhead is moving *forward* parallel to the ground. Therefore, the ball must spin because the blow is glancing (principle 1). The blow is glancing because the clubface is looking in a different direction (upward) than the clubhead is moving (forward), which is principle 2. This spin will cause the ball to curve upward in the direction the clubface was looking instead of forward in the direction the clubhead was moving (principle 3). The amount it will spin upward depends, in part, on the difference between the club's upward facing and its forward movement, or, in this case, upon the club's degree of loft (principle 4).

In this example I have, in effect, described a good golf shot. As we've explained, all good golf shots have some degree of backspin that causes the ball to rise and remain for a while in the air.

Example 2: Same conditions as in example 1, except that the clubhead is moving upward instead of parallel to the ground during impact.

In this case, since the clubhead is moving upward, in somewhat the same direction that its loft causes it to face, there is *less difference* be-

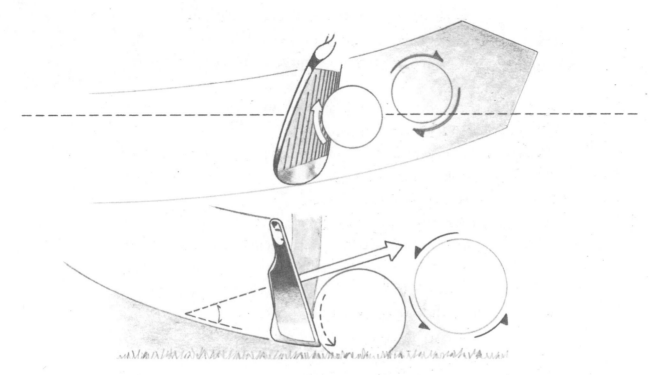

For a golf shot to curve sideways, the ball must take on some sidespin. For it to maintain itself in the air for any appreciable distance, it must also backspin. Both sidespin and backspin can occur only when a glancing blow is applied to the ball. A glancing blow can occur only when the clubface is looking in a different direction that it is moving at the time it releases the ball. Here we see two examples of clubheads applying spin because the blow is glancing, because the clubfaces are looking in a different direction than they are moving. In the first instance we see sidespin being applied because the clubface is looking to the right while moving to the left. In the second case we see backspin applied because the clubface is looking (lofted) upward while it is moving slightly downward.

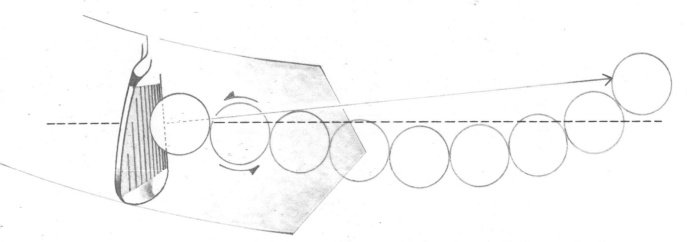

Once spin is applied to the ball, the shot will tend to curve in the direction the clubface was looking at impact, and away from the direction it was moving. Here we see a clubhead that is looking to the left of where it is moving. Thus the ball will eventually curve to the left.

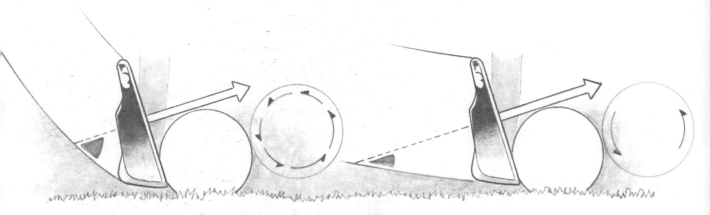

The greater the difference between the direction the clubface is looking and the path on which it is moving during impact, the greater the amount of spin it will apply to the ball. Here we see two clubheads making contact. The clubhead on the left is moving more sharply downward than the clubhead on the right. Thus the difference between its path of movement and its direction of facing is greater. Thus it will apply more backspin to the ball. Wise golfers apply this knowledge by striking downward to make shots fly high and by swinging slightly upward—usually on tee shots—to make the ball bore lower. Many novice players mistakenly swing upward to make the ball fly higher, and merely dribble it along the ground through failure to apply backspin.

tween its facing and its path of movement. Therefore, because of principle 4, this decreased difference produces *less* spin and less upward curve.

This example is extremely important in that many golfers seem to think that they must scoop upward—swing *up* to the ball—to get it into the air. As we see here, such an upward clubhead path actually *reduces* spin and *decreases* the height of the shot. So never try to scoop shots upward. Instead, rely on the club's built-in loft to make the ball fly into the air.

---

*"I was a member of Grout's Friday morning class when I was 11 and 12. By my second summer, I had become his prize demonstrator. 'Jackie,' he would say, 'come out here and show us what it means to hit down on the ball.' I'd trot out and hit a few shots emphatically on the downswing and, after some complimentary remark by Grout, trot back to my place."—*JACK NICKLAUS

Example 3: Same conditions as in example 1, except that the clubhead path is slightly downward during impact.

Here, because of the clubhead's slightly downward path of movement, there is a *greater* difference between it and the upward facing of the clubface. This greater difference causes *more* backspin and *more* height (principle 4).

This example helps to explain why good golfers try to hit iron shots while the clubhead is still moving *slightly* downward, before it reaches the bottom of its arc and starts upward. (You will note that these players, as a result, remove turf—take a divot—*in front* of the ball's original position on many iron shots.) Striking the ball with a slightly downward-moving clubhead gives the good golfer more backspin, which tends to offset any sidespin that might cause the ball to curve off line. The downward blow, along with the tremendous clubhead speed these better golfers achieve, also explains why their shots often spin backward after landing.

This example also illustrates one of the advantages Jack Nicklaus has over most of his opponents as the result of developing a relatively upright swing. This type of swing causes the clubhead to move into the ball at a slightly steeper angle of attack, which produces more backspin, which results in added height. Such height is especially helpful on long shots to a green in that, by descending at a sharper angle, the ball quickly settles close to where it lands, instead of driving low and forward and scooting over the putting surface.

Example 4: Clubhead path is across the line from the outside to the inside. Clubface looks down the line during impact.

Here we find spin applied because the blow is glancing (principle 1). The blow is glancing because the club faces in a different direction than it is moving (principle 2). The shot curves to the right because the clubface is looking to the right of where the club is moving (principle 3).

This example describes the typical "slice" pattern that most golfers apply to most of their shots. Actually, the ball starts to the left of target because that is the direction in which the clubhead is moving, then side-spin takes over and causes the ball to curve back to the right.

This is a weak blow, first because it is a glancing blow, and secondly because the outside-inside clubhead path causes too steep an angle of attack, making the application of force too much downward instead of forward.

Again, this slice pattern will produce less sidespin curve with the highly-lofted clubs, because the increased backspin they tend to apply overcomes much of the sidespin. Golfers who slice their drives thus generally tend to pull their short shots to the left, because that is the direction—in both cases—in which they are swinging the clubhead at impact.

By now you should be getting familiar with the four principles of spin and how they affect golf shots. There are many other examples, but the principles remain the same.

If, for instance, your clubhead was moving from outside to inside the line during impact, but the face looked to the left of this path, your shot would start left of target (in the direction the clubhead was moving) and spin further left (in the direction the clubface was looking).

If your clubhead was moving down the target line but facing right or left of it, your shot would curve right or left respectively. If the path were inside-to-outside across the line, the ball would start out to the right but then curve either left or further right if the face were looking left or right of this path of movement.

These are the "ballistics" of golf. If you understand them, you will be forever able to look at your shots and determine immediately what might be causing them to fly left or right, or too high or too low.

"Many mature golfers—mature in years, I mean— probably do not understand cause-and-effect factors—the spin factors—that are so obvious to me that I apply them automatically in my own game today. I once got into a discussion with a pro-am partner about his slice, a really wicked monster that was obviously ruining his golfing life. He'd tried just about every method and gimmick ever invented. But what he'd obviously failed to comprehend were the simple, basic mechanics of impact— what causes a ball to fly a certain way. He was forever changing his swing without really considering what he wanted it to achieve for him at impact."— JACK NICKLAUS

CHAPTER FOUR

*The Six Fundamentals
You Should Master*

"I like to go back to Jack Grout every year. That's partly because I simply enjoy seeing Jack, but also because I feel you really need someone to bring you down to earth with the basic fundamentals of what the game of golf is all about.

"I ask Jack, 'How's my grip?' Well, the average golfer might laugh his head off if he saw Jack Nicklaus walk in and ask someone about his grip. But I'm serious; a man's grip can change over a period of time. So can his head position, his ball position, and so on. Checking out my fundamentals this way gets me started off right at the beginning of every year."—JACK NICKLAUS

I've never met a beginner with more natural talent than Jack Nicklaus had from the start. And I've never known anyone so determined to excel at golf. But the main reason for Jack's success is neither talent nor desire; it's mainly his total adherence to the fundamentals.

Sticking with the basics through thick and thin has given Jack's swing a tremendous repetitiveness. Today it is almost identical to the swing he used in winning the U.S. Amateur Championship as a 19-year-old. The only major difference is that today he can, if he wishes, stand slightly closer to the ball—a result of his learning to live without his once-beloved mashed potatoes and gravy!

A solid bedrock of fundamentals also gives you tremendous confidence in your technique. And, just as important, it gives you something to fall back on when the going gets rough. In my opinion, no one in the past 50 years—since the Walter Hagen era—has been Jack's equal when it comes to *winning* tournaments while playing relatively *bad* golf.

As I've said, in many ways golf is the most *unnatural* game in the world. For this reason *natural* ability will take you only so far. At some point your progress will hit a dead end unless you have sound swing fundamentals. But when you have them, you can continue to improve over the years for as long as you want to work on executing them better and better.

ADVICE TO JUNIORS

Both Jack and I have witnessed countless junior golfers with a lot of promise who managed to shoot lower and lower scores until they were about 18 years old. Then, gradually, their scores began to level off, or even start climbing higher. What happened was that these youngsters either didn't understand certain swing fundamentals or weren't willing to put forth much effort to develop them. Instead, they tried this or that gimmick until they had so many different ways to swing the club that they never knew which one to use.

ADVICE TO ADULTS

In trying to play golf well you will be tempted to read all the "tips" you can find in the magazines, and also probably to listen to various friends' well-meant suggestions. While many of these tips may be valid for some golfers, only a very small fraction will apply to your particular needs. The rest will do you more harm than good. Therefore, I suggest that, after having learned as much as you can about basic golf concepts, such as those in the previous chapter, and about swing fundamentals, such as those that follow, you become highly selective about what specific instruction you apply to your swing. Sticking only to those suggestions that obviously will enhance your ability to execute a basic fundamental is an excellent policy, and one that Jack Nicklaus has always resolutely followed.

The six fundamentals that follow are the same ones that I taught Jack Nicklaus, Sr., am now teaching Jack Nicklaus, Jr., and would no doubt teach you if I had you face to face on the lesson tee. I present them to you as a base on which to build your game. Though few in number, they cover all vital areas of the golf swing. Learn them well and you will have developed an outstanding swing.

I must tell you in all honesty, however, that learning to apply these, or any other, golf fundamentals properly and consistently always requires effort. I feel that it takes a beginning junior golfer about five years, practicing three or four times a week, to implant all of these fundamentals to the point where they are second nature. For an adult beginner, the period would be *at least* five years. And thereafter, like Jack Nicklaus, he or she would need to play and practice fairly regularly—say twice a week—merely to maintain these skills.

69

Perhaps you are not willing to make such an all-out effort. Perhaps you will settle for whatever level of skill you can develop over a period of, say, a few weeks. The degree of effort is up to you, of course. My only hope is that whatever effort you do make will be devoted strictly to the fundamentals that I present here. In that way, I feel, you will be getting the most value from your investment of time and energy.

FUNDAMENTAL 1: Set Up Correctly

It was the 1974 U.S. Open at Winged Foot, Mamaroneck, New York, and I was watching Jack Nicklaus warm up on the practice range before one of his rounds. I can't recall ever seeing him swing so badly.

Jack didn't realize it at the time, but he was obviously setting up to his shots (addressing the ball) with an extremely "closed" shoulder alignment. By that I mean that his upper body was aligned so that, if you laid a club across his chest, the shaft would point far to the right of his target. In fact, there was a fence running down the right side of the range, and his shoulders were aligned even to the right of that.

Now, the last thing you want to do to a friend is to start him thinking about changing his swing just a few minutes before he's supposed to tee it up in the National Open. However, Jack's bad alignment was forcing him to make such a screwball swing in order to get his shots going anywhere near to his target that I figured I couldn't put him into any worse shape. If he were to hit his shots in the direction he was aligned, the ball would finish far to the right of every fairway and green on the course.

So I asked him, "Jack, where are you aiming?"

"At that tree," he answered, pointing down the center of the range.

"See that fence over there on the right?" I asked. "Well, as far as

I'm concerned that is 'out of bounds'. And you are aiming your shoulders to the *right* of that fence."

I guess he decided he didn't want to change things at that time, but a few days later we were standing on the sixth tee of the Memorial Course he has built at Muirfield Village Golf Club in Columbus, Ohio. Jack was getting set up to drive and he was still aligning his shoulders way out to the right.

I went up to him, grabbed his shoulders, and turned them around so that they were just a little "open"—aligned slightly *left* of the center of the fairway. Of course, that new alignment felt just terrible to Jack, as I knew it would.

"I can't hit it from here," he said. "I'll go way over there to the left."

"Just let it go over there," I told him.

With that he made a swing and hit the ball—"bam"—right down the center of the fairway. Then he hit some more drives with his new shoulder alignment. Bam! Bam! Bam! Every ball split the fairway like a bullet.

I know Jack won't mind my mentioning this incident because it makes the point that setting up correctly is all-important, and that it's all too easy—even for the world's greatest golfer—to fall into a bad setup pattern. And I am harping on the point because I want you to understand that nothing has more to do with the success or failure of your shots than the way you position your club and yourself before you swing.

"I am sometimes accused of being a slow player. Well, the truth is that I walk very fast up to the ball, make a fairly fast decision about what I want to do when I get there, but then sometimes set up to the shot slowly.

"There are some good reasons for my being so methodical about my setup. I think it is the single most important maneuver in golf. It is the only aspect of the swing over which you have 100 percent control. If you set up correctly, there's a good chance you'll hit a reasonable shot, even if you make a mediocre swing. If you set up incorrectly, you'll hit a lousy shot even if you make the greatest swing in the world.

"Every time I try to deny that law by hurrying my setup, my subconscious rears up and beats me around the ears."—JACK NICKLAUS

I doubt that five percent of those who play golf have good address positions, even though many know that the address position actually determines *how* they will swing the club, for good or for bad. However, those who do are, almost to the man (or woman), outstanding players.

Learning to set up correctly isn't very exciting. Perhaps that's why we see so few golfers with good setups. However, I really hope that I can persuade you to master this fundamental before you go any farther into learning golf. With a good setup, everything else will fall into place much, much more quickly and more easily. Without a good setup, the odds are heavily against your ever becoming much of a golfer.

The fundamentals of a proper setup include both aiming the club and positioning yourself. Aiming comes first because so much about positioning yourself relates to where you initially set and face your clubhead.

For instance, if you should happen to misaim the club far to the right of your target—as a surprising number of golfers actually do—two things can happen. One possibility would be that you would align your-self in the same direction that you misaimed the clubface, and then actu-ally swing the club where you've aimed both it and yourself. If you then make square contact, the ball will finish far to the right of your target. (Actually, this result would not be too bad in the long run, because you would soon tire of hitting your best shots far to the right, and, instead, would subconsciously start aiming both the club and yourself more to the left, or more toward where you should have been aiming in the first place.)

A more common reaction to aiming the club and yourself to the right, however, would be to subconsciously pull the club back to the left —toward the actual target—on your downswing. Aiming right and swinging left would thus cause you to swing your clubhead across your target line, from outside to inside, during impact. This path would nor-mally deliver a glancing blow sideways at too steep an angle of attack, causing the shot to fly low and curve weakly from left to right.

Good golfers set the clubhead behind the ball and aim it on target *before* they adjust their feet and body into position. This makes sense because it is easier to aim your club correctly than it is to aim yourself without the clubhead for reference. You are thus more likely to finish with a good aim *and* a good setup if you base your setup on where you've aimed the club, instead of aiming the club according to where, for good or for bad, you've happened to set your feet and aligned your body.

Aiming the club is something that requires periodic checking. As even Nicklaus finds, its oh so easy to start misaiming right or left. When-ever you practice, try to find someone to stand behind your ball, looking down your target line, to check your aim.

Or lay another club on the ground a few feet in front of your ball and pointing down your target line, then aim the clubface down the line formed by the club on the ground. As you do so, also check your distant

AIMING THE CLUBFACE *is vastly important yet surprisingly difficult for most golfers. Even touring professional must periodically check to see that they are getting the correct visual impression as they aim. One way to do this is to first lay a club on the ground pointing toward a given target. Next, aim your clubface down the clubshaft. Finally, check the positioning of your clubface as it relates to your original, distant target. Though you know your clubface is aimed at this target, it may appear to be aiming left or right of it. If so, you must nevertheless abide with this distortion—and try to reproduce a similar distortion—on all your normal shots. In time you will learn to trust the fact that you must feel misaimed in order to be properly aimed.*

target and note how your clubface looks, or seems to look, in relation to it. By doing this you will gradually discover exactly how your clubface should really look to you when it is, in fact, aimed squarely at the target.

Once you have aimed your club on target and soled the bottom of it flat on the ground, you should set yourself in position by using the ball and the clubhead and the handle of the club as guides. The exact procedure for doing this follows. It may seem like a great deal to digest all at once, but you must take the time to master the procedure if you hope ever to become a decent golfer. So don't rush it.

To master proper setup procedure, I suggest that you now take a club (a 5 iron is ideal), a ball, and a yardstick. Stand in front of a mirror. As you move yourself into the positions that follow, check yourself in the mirror. Compare yourself with the drawings that accompany this chapter.

In time, you will find it easier and easier to move directly into a proper address position almost subconsciously—you'll learn to "find" the right setup by "feeling" it. Once you can do this quickly and almost automatically and, upon rechecking in the mirror find yourself correctly positioned, you will be a long way down the road toward becoming an excellent golfer. For the moment, however, take your time and be very specific in following this procedure:

1. Place the ball on the floor and select a "target line" running from it to some object in the mirror.

2. Hold the club in both hands and place the clubhead behind the ball so that it faces squarely down your target line. As you look down at it, the forward edge of the clubhead—the bottom edge of the clubface—should square off with the target line itself. (Don't worry about how you hold the club at this point—that will come later. But *do* put your right hand just below your left on the shaft if you are righthanded.)

3. Place your left foot in position so that: (a) a line running along

STEP 1—*Take out a yardstick, your 5 iron and a ball. Place the ball in front of a mirror. Select a target line from the ball to some object that appears in the mirror.*

STEP 2—*Holding the club in both hands, but with your right below your left on the shaft, place the clubhead behind the ball, facing down your target line. The leading, or bottom, edge of the clubface should square with your target line.*

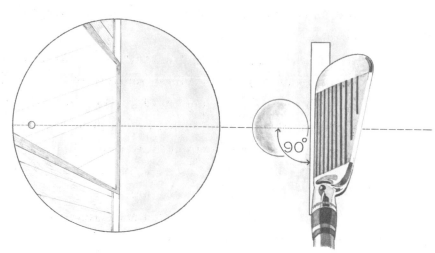

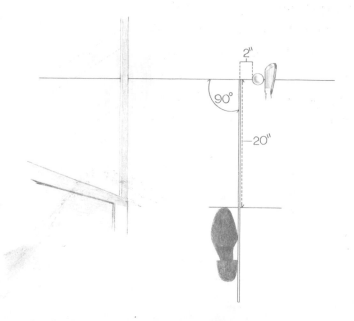

STEP 3—*Place your left toe 20 inches from your target line with your foot in position so that a line running along its inside edge would intersect your target line at 90 degrees and at a point two inches left of the ball. (Use your yardstick for precise measuring.)*

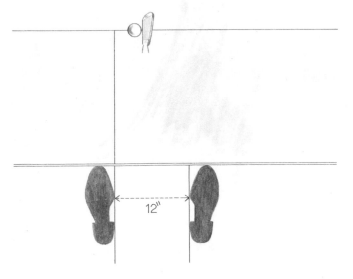

STEP 4—*Place your right foot in position so that it aligns with your left, is 12 inches from it and an equal distance (20 inches) from your target line. A line across your toes would run parallel to your target line. (When your toe line is thus parallel, your stance is considered "square." When your toe line extends away from your target line, your stance is called "open." It is "closed" when your toe line extends towards your target line.)*

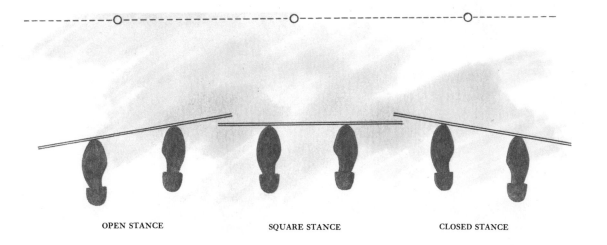

OPEN STANCE   **SQUARE STANCE**   **CLOSED STANCE**

STEP 5—*Swivel your left heel two inches to the right and your right heel one inch to your left. At this point practice stepping back from, and then re-entering, your stance. Do so until you can consistently step into the correct positions. Then proceed to the next page.*

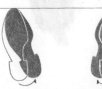

STEP 6—*With your feet correctly positioned (see preceding pages), stand perfectly upright with the club extended horizontally at arms' length.*

STEP 7—*Bending only from your hips, lower the clubhead into position behind the ball.*

STEP 8—*Flex your knees slightly by simply lowering your buttocks until a line across your knees would run parallel to your toe line and about two inches to your side of it.*

STEP 9—*Distribute your weight more or less equally between your feet and between the ball and heel of each foot.*

STEP 10—*Align your hips and chest so that lines across each would run parallel to your target line, toe line and knee line. This gives you an overall "square" alignment. (Small figure at lower-left shows variations in alignment, with toe line square hip line "open" and shoulder or chest line "closed.") Check to see that your overall view from the side looks like the golfer shown in the larger drawing.*

STEP 11—*Turn to face mirror and check to see that your overall face-on view resembles figure shown here. Note that this golfer's left side is somewhat lower than his right, because his left hand is lower on the clubshaft. Hands should be just slightly ahead of the clubhead, with your head largely behind the ball.*

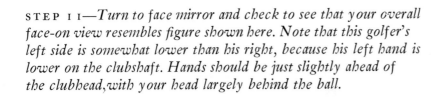

its inside edge would intersect at a 90° ("square") angle with your target line, at (b) a point two inches to the left of the ball, and (c) so that your big toe is 20 inches from your target line.

4. Place your right foot in position so that: (a) it sets parallel to your left foot, (b) there is a 12-inch space between your feet, and (c) a line across the toes of each shoe runs parallel to your target line. (When these lines are parallel, your stance is considered "square." It is "open" if your toeline, when extended forward to the mirror, would point away from your target line, and "closed" if it would eventually cross it.)

5. Swivel your left heel two inches to the right, toward your right heel. Swivel your right heel one inch to the left.

At this point, study your foot positioning and try to memorize how it looks in relation to the ball and your clubhead. Then step back from the ball and re-enter your stance. See how closely you can come to properly placing your feet. Continue doing this until it becomes natural for you to: (a) place your clubhead in proper position behind the ball, (b) step into proper position with your left foot, and (c) adjust your right foot into its proper position. This is the routine for stepping into position that you should follow on the course for as long as you play golf.

6. Having stepped into the foot positions described thus far, but this time *not* putting your clubhead behind the ball, stand perfectly upright with the club in both hands and extended horizontally at arms length in front of you. Your arms should be straight, but not stiff or tense.

7. Bending *only from your hips*, not from your upper back or neck, lower the clubhead into position behind the ball.

8. Flex your knees slightly by simply lowering your buttocks, making a sitting down motion until a line across the tips of your knees would: (a) parallel a line across your toes, and (b) run about two inches inside it.

9. Distribute your weight more or less equally between your feet, and between the ball and heel of each foot.

10. Align your hips and chest so that a line across each would run parallel to your target line, your toe line and your knee line. Once all these lines are parallel you will have set up "square" overall. If any of these lines should extend away from or across your target line, that part of your anatomy would be considered "open" or "closed" respectively, rather than "square."

11. Slide your hands and the top of the clubshaft left or right—toward or away from your target—until your left arm and your clubshaft form a fairly straight line from your left shoulder to the ball. (Important: you may raise or lower your left shoulder and side as you slide your hands left or right, but be sure not to open or close your body alignment as you do so.)

At this point you should be set up correctly for making a proper golf swing. Check, however, to see if your image in the mirror looks like the face-on and side-view drawings shown on these pages. Make sure, for instance, that your head and neck haven't slumped forward, and that your back is still straight. You will also note that your right side, shoulder and hip, is slightly lower than your left. This is normal, largely because your right hand is lower than your left on the clubshaft.

Again, practice moving into this over-all address position for as long as it takes for you to do so naturally and correctly. Continually check to make sure that you have followed each point I've detailed. In fact, since it is so easy unknowingly to fall out of proper address position, you should periodically check yourself in the mirror, against this list, as long as you play golf.

The positioning I've given you is that which I feel is ideal for most golfers on full shots with a 5 iron. For swings with a different club, the only variations from the dimensions I've just outlined will be (a) in the distance you stand from your target line, and (b) in the space between your feet. All other aspects of aim and setup apply to all normal, full shots with all clubs.

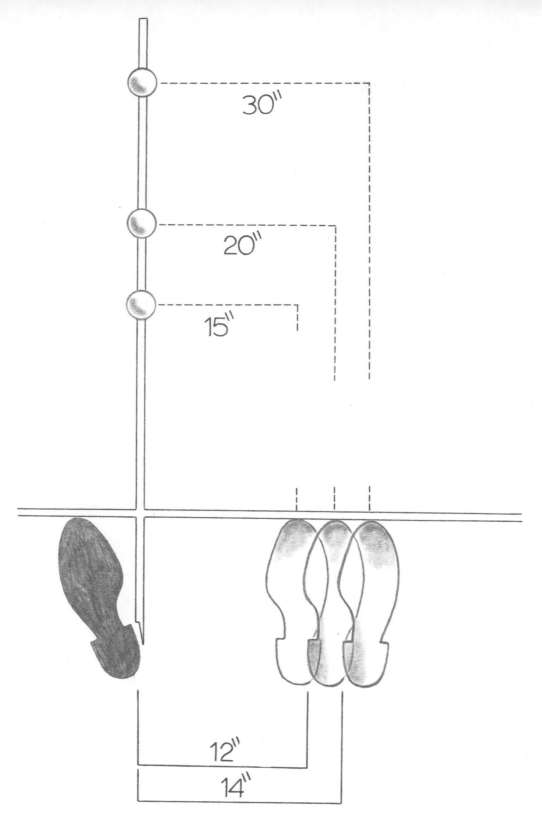

THE IDEAL STANCE WIDTH *and distance from the ball varies with the length of club being used. However, for most golfers the distance between the feet on drives should not exceed 14 inches or the distance from the ball to the toe line 30 inches. The distance from the ball to the toe line decreases to about 20 inches for the 5 iron and 15 inches for a full shot with a pitching wedge. Maximum stance width for a 5 iron is 12 inches, measured from the innermost side of each foot, and gradually less for shorter shots. All shots are played with the ball more or less opposite the inside of the left heel, but novice players may play it an inch or two more towards stance-center until they develop proper foot and legwork.*

You should stand progressively farther than 20 inches from your target line for shots with longer-shafted clubs, and progressively closer as you move into the shorter irons. However, you should *never* set your toes farther than 30 inches from your target line, even with your longest club, the driver, unless you happen to be unusually stout. Then you might stand 31 or 32 inches away, but no farther.

Your stance should widen slightly for shots with longer clubs so that you can maintain good balance despite the longer swing they will encourage you to make automatically. However, even with a No. 1 wood, you should never widen your stance more than an additional two inches. Naturally, you can gradually narrow your stance on shots with shorter clubs, where you'll be making shorter and less forceful swings that require less stance width for maintaining balance.

I must state here that no two golfers are exactly alike in build or type of swing. Therefore, a golf professional who teaches you face to face might prescribe for you personally a slight variation from the setup that I've outlined here. You should heed his advice, since he has the advantage of seeing your physique and swing pattern firsthand. I do feel, however, that the setup I've outlined, if followed to the letter, will give you a far better address position, and thus a much better chance to excel at golf, than that now being used by the vast majority of those with whom you play, both now and in the future.

Finally, let me stress once again the importance of learning to set up to the ball smoothly and without delay. At first you will need to check each of the various points I've mentioned while you are settling over the ball. In time, however, this should become unnecessary: you should eventually be able to step quickly into the correct position, waggle the club, and get on with your swing. The longer you stand over the ball, and the more things that you consciously flash through your head, the less chance you'll have of making a smooth, rhythmical swing.

FUNDAMENTAL 2: A Proper Grip

To me, the hands are a necessary evil in golf. You need them to hold onto the club, but beyond that they usually do far more harm than good.

Consciously trying to use your hands and wrists to either add distance or make better contact with the ball usually has just the opposite effect: you either waste clubhead speed, or throw or shove the clubhead off line, or both. The best thing you can do with your hands as you swing is nothing. Simply hold on and let them react naturally to the weight and movement of the club itself.

If this is true, then a good grip is one that lets you make square contact with your maximum clubhead speed while you are simply holding onto the club. A bad grip is one that forces you to grab with, throw with, push with, or otherwise manipulate your hands as you swing. It's my strongly-held opinion that at least 90 percent of the world's golfers have bad grips that cost them both distance and accuracy.

There are three specific requirements of a good grip.

The first is that you hold the club with just enough pressure to control it throughout the swing, including the moment of impact, but never so much that you inhibit free swinging. Most golfers either grip too tightly from the time they first address the ball, or they grab hold of the club tightly, usually with their "throwing" hand, some time prior to impact.

Your grip pressure will change automatically to some degree as you swing, especially in that it must increase gradually as the clubhead picks up speed. However, this change should be subtle, gradual, and unconscious. Sudden grabbing inhibits free swinging of the arms, free hinging and unhinging of the wrists, and, in consequence, free squaring of the clubface through impact.

THE FIRST REQUIREMENT FOR A GOOD GRIP *is that you hold the club with proper pressure. This is necessary for club control and free swinging. Too little pressure allows slippage, which is usually followed immediately by sudden clenching. Such rapid and dramatic changes in pressure while swinging inhibit free squaring of the clubface by impact and stifle the full buildup and release of clubhead speed. Start with no more pressure than you need merely to hold the clubhead off the ground. As you swing, the weight of the moving club will force you instinctively to grip firmer, but you should avoid any sudden grabbing.*

I cannot tell you exactly how firmly to hold the club, because this varies with the individual. I do suggest, though, that you start with no more overall grip pressure than you need to merely hold the clubhead an inch or so off the ground. Thereafter, as you swing, add only enough pressure to keep the club from slipping in your hands.

The second requirement of a good grip is that it allows your hands to work together as a unit instead of as two opposing forces. For your hands to work together, they must: (a) join each other snugly, (b) take up as little space on the club as possible, and (c) align together with the palms more or less facing each other.

There are three basic types of grip that join the hands together on the club. They are similar in that each finds the thumb of the left hand resting in the palm of the right. They vary, however, in the way they relate the forefinger of the left hand and the little finger of the right in a "knitting together" action.

In the so-called "ten-finger" grip, these two fingers curl around the club side by side, but they do not otherwise join together. This type of grip gets its name because all ten fingers are on the club, and it is probably the least popular of the three grips, largely, I feel, because it takes up more space on the club than do the other two. The more space your grip requires, the more likely your hands are to work independently of each other.

The so-called "interlock" grip twines the little finger on the right hand between the forefinger and middle finger of the left. This is the grip that Jack Nicklaus uses and strongly advocates. Some excellent golfers have interlocked—Sarazen, Picard, Mangrum, MacFarlane, Mahaffey, for example—and it does provide a snug linking of the hands, which makes the style especially useful for people with small or relatively weak hands.

By far the most popular grip, used and advocated by at least nine out

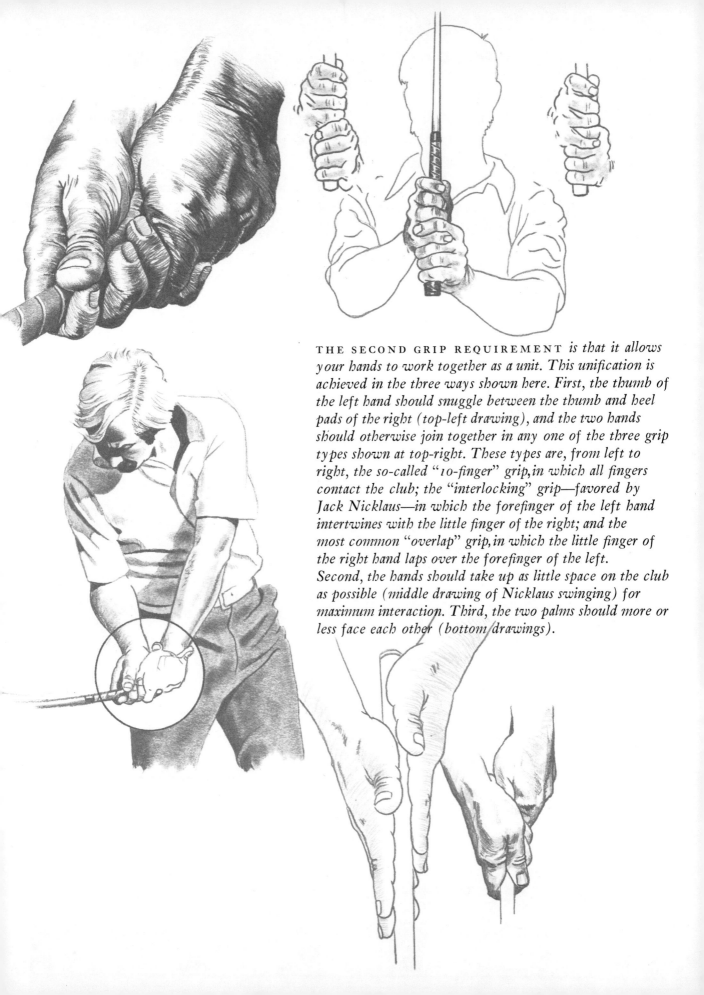

THE SECOND GRIP REQUIREMENT *is that it allows your hands to work together as a unit. This unification is achieved in the three ways shown here. First, the thumb of the left hand should snuggle between the thumb and heel pads of the right (top-left drawing), and the two hands should otherwise join together in any one of the three grip types shown at top-right. These types are, from left to right, the so-called "10-finger" grip, in which all fingers contact the club; the "interlocking" grip—favored by Jack Nicklaus—in which the forefinger of the left hand intertwines with the little finger of the right; and the most common "overlap" grip, in which the little finger of the right hand laps over the forefinger of the left. Second, the hands should take up as little space on the club as possible (middle drawing of Nicklaus swinging) for maximum interaction. Third, the two palms should more or less face each other (bottom drawings).*

of ten golf pros, is the "overlap" grip (sometimes called the "Vardon" grip in that it was popularized by the great British player, Harry Vardon, in the late 19th century). In this grip, the little finger of the right hand laps over the forefinger of the left hand instead of intertwining with it. When Jack Nicklaus was a boy he played some 50 rounds with the overlap grip, but then returned to interlocking, which he found more securely united his comparatively small hands.

Whichever grip you choose, be sure that your hands *never* separate during your swing. This would force you to regrip before impact and thereby almost certainly to throw the clubhead off line. A light but constant nudging of your left-hand thumb pad against your right-hand heel pad will counter any such separation.

Finally, for your hands to work as a unit, they must more or less align with each other on the club. This means that if you were to open your hands after having assumed your grip, you would find that your palms were facing each other.

The third basic grip requirement is that your hold on the club allows you naturally and unconsciously to square its face at impact whenever you swing your arms and turn yourself back and through as freely as possible.

The direction in which your club will face at impact is largely determined by the direction in which your hands face after you have completed your grip. Assuming that you put your hands on the club with the palms facing, as suggested, you will find that, generally speaking, the more your right palm faces *downward* at address, the more your clubface will be looking to the *right* of target at impact. Conversely, the more your right palm faces *upward* at address, the greater your chances for a clubface that looks to the *left* of target on impact. Thus, setting the hands to the left at address causes shots to curve to the right, and setting them to the right causes shots to curve to the left. Bearing this in mind,

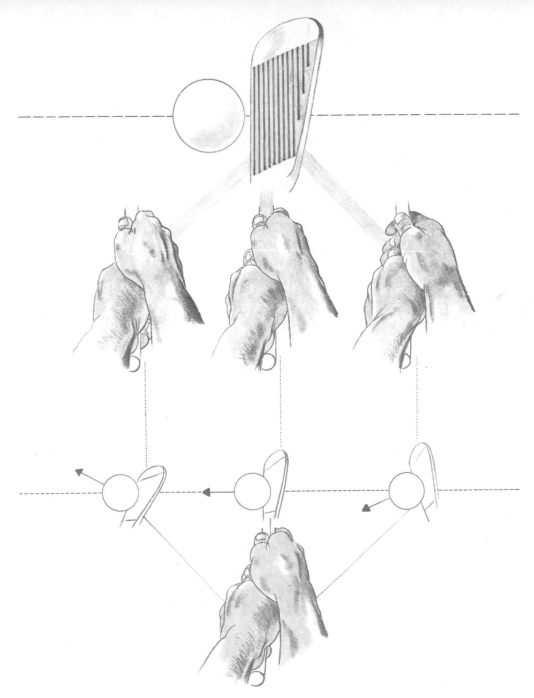

THE THIRD GRIP REQUIREMENT *is that you position your hands on the club at address in a way that allows them to square the clubface to the line during impact when you swing freely. As a general rule, when you square your clubface to the line at address (top clubhead drawing) and set your hands on the club so they are turned far to your left (see hands on the left), you will tend to return the clubface to impact in an "open" position (see clubhead on the left) and slice your shots to the right. This occurs because your hands will tend to return to a neutral position at impact (bottom set of hands) instead of to their original address position. If you turn your hands too far to your right at address (see hands on the right), and return again to the neutral hand position at impact, your clubface will be facing to the left (see clubhead on the right) and you will hook your shots. Somewhere between these two extremes is a neutral address-position grip (middle set of hands, for example) to which you can regularly return at impact and thereby square your clubface to the line. To find the position that is correct for you, position your hands more to your left at address if your shots are now curving to the left, or more to your right if they are now curving right.*

experiment with various grip positionings until you find the one that most frequently gives you the "shape" of shot you desire when you swing freely.

Thus, to summarize our second fundamental, on proper gripping, you should hold the club with your hands: (a) facing, (b) unified, (c) positioned to allow free squaring of the clubface, and (d) just firmly enough to maintain control.

ADVICE TO JUNIORS

I find that youngsters frequently try to copy the grips of experts, which places the palms more or less parallel with the clubface and faces the back of the left hand and the palm of the right hand directly forward rather than upward or downward. While this positioning is ideal for certain adults, until you put on a little more golfing muscle it may not give you enough left-hand control of the club as you swing.

If you find that you either let go of the club at the top of your backswing or slice your shots from left to right, you should set your hands on the club when gripping so that they are both turned slightly farther to your right—in other words, your right palm and the back of your left hand should face slightly *upward*. As you get older and stronger, or if you start hooking shots to the left, you can gradually set your hands farther to the left.

FUNDAMENTAL 3: Steady Head

"I regard keeping the head very steady, if not absolutely stock still, throughout the swing as THE

bedrock fundamental of golf. . . . If you can't or won't learn to keep your head steady . . . there is nothing that I or anyone else can do for your golf game."—JACK NICKLAUS

Your head is the hub or axis of your swing, around which you both turn your torso and swing your club. And, in that role, more than any other part of your anatomy it can, if improperly used, totally ruin your swing. Properly used, on the other hand, it can offset a multitude of swing errors.

Ideally, you should position your head slightly behind the ball as you set up to your shot. Put your left cheek about even with the back of the ball. Next, just before you start your backswing, turn your chin an inch or two toward your right shoulder. Finally, hold that head position until *after* you have hit the ball, when the momentum of your swing will force your chin to rotate to your left.

Sounds simple? I suppose it does. Maybe it will be for you, but it certainly wasn't for Jack Nicklaus.

"I believe that keeping the head still is one of the most difficult things a golfer has to learn to do. Certainly it was for me. . . . When nothing else would work he (Jack Grout) had his assistant, Larry Glosser, stand in front of me and grab my hair while I hit shots. My scalp still tingles at the thought of those sessions. I cried tears of pain many a time. But by the time I was 13 I had learned

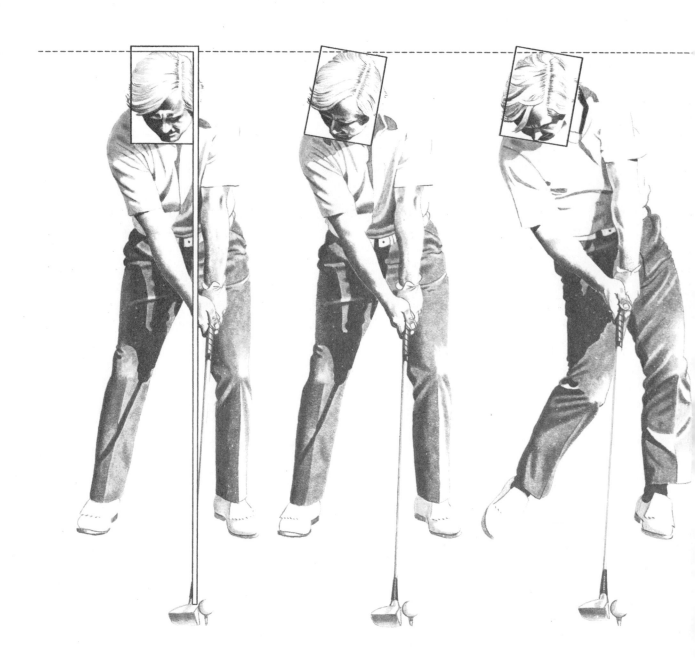

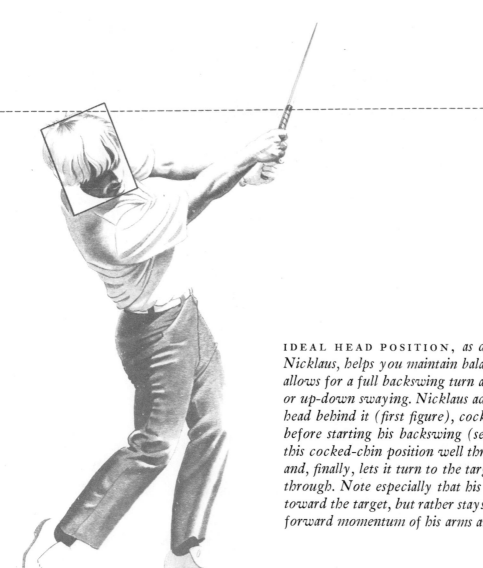

IDEAL HEAD POSITION, *as demonstrated by Jack Nicklaus, helps you maintain balance while you swing. It also allows for a full backswing turn and disallows any sideways or up-down swaying. Nicklaus addresses the ball with his head behind it (first figure), cocks his chin to his right just before starting his backswing (second figure), maintains this cocked-chin position well through impact (third figure) and, finally, lets it turn to the target as his shoulders turn through. Note especially that his head never slides forward toward the target, but rather stays back to counter balance the forward momentum of his arms and club.*

to keep my head in one place, no matter how hard I tried to hit the ball."—JACK NICKLAUS

Turning your head to your right and then keeping it steady—not rigid—until after impact causes many good things to happen in your golf swing, such as:

• It helps you to start the club back slowly and smoothly.

• It clears the way for your shoulders to turn fully and freely on your backswing.

• It helps to produce a full, springlike coiling of your muscles during your backswing, for greater build-up of potential clubhead speed.

• It disallows any sideways or up-down swaying that might distort your swing path and arc, or inhibit full coiling.

• It helps you to maintain balance as you swing.

• It sets and keeps your eyes in position for you to "see" the proper path along which your clubhead should approach the ball (from inside to along the target line).

Taken as a whole, these plus factors add up to longer, straighter shots and greater overall shotmaking consistency.

The best way to check for head movement is simply to ask a friend to watch you swing. Another way is to finish hitting a shot and then merely *turn* your head back to look at where the ball was originally. Do not lower, lift or slide it sideways as you do so, but after turning it back simply check to see if it is still setting where it was when you addressed the ball.

Yet another way to check for head movement is to position yourself so that the shadow of your head at address covers a certain leaf or, perhaps, the ball itself. Then hit practice shots and notice if the shadow of your head moves off the spot as you swing.

I seriously doubt that you will ever reach the point where your head doesn't shift slightly at some point during most of your swings. Studies of touring professionals have shown some slight head movement even in their case—usually slightly down and away from the target on the forward swing. The message I want to leave with you, however, is that even though you may never achieve perfection with this particular fundamental, the closer you come to it as you develop your golf game, the better you will play for the rest of your life.

FUNDAMENTAL 4: *Proper Footwork*

"I was taught to play, and still do play, from the 'insides' of my feet. This was an insurance against losing balance or swaying my head or upper body while hitting the ball hard."—JACK NICKLAUS

One of the main things that makes good golfers good is their ability to keep themselves in balance while they swing full out. You see many mediocre players, especially older adults, who do stay nicely in balance but don't really create much motion: all they basically do is lift the club up and down with their hands and arms. And you see many other poor players who make all kinds of motion—arms, shoulders, hips, legs, everything moves—but who fall all over themselves by losing balance: no two swings they make are anywhere near similar.

As I've mentioned, keeping a steady head while swinging does help you to maintain balance. However, it is proper footwork that primarily

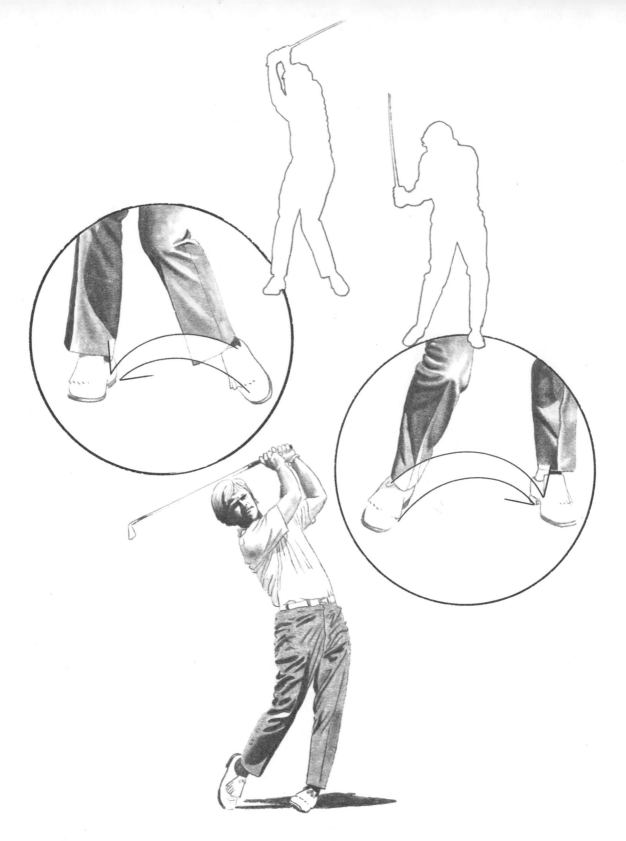

PROPER FOOTWORK *is primarily a matter of rolling the ankles so that weight shifts to and from the insides of the feet. During the backswing, roll your left ankle to the right so that most of your weight feels like it has shifted onto the inside of your right foot. At the start of your downswing, roll your right ankle to the left so that weight shifts onto your left foot. Continue this shifting until you finish your swing with almost all your weight on your left foot. Keep both knees flexed slightly throughout. Such footwork not only improves balance but also adds rhythm and force to your swing.*

promotes both balance *and* full swinging. And once you develop proper footwork, I can promise you that you'll hit your shots both farther and more accurately, and that you'll do so a lot more consistently.

Proper footwork is simply a matter of rolling your ankles correctly while keeping your knees flexed at all times. On the backswing your left ankle rolls inward toward your right foot, so that most of your weight shifts from left to right onto the *inside* of the right foot (the rest remaining on the inside of the left). Then, at the start of your downswing, *both* ankles roll laterally to the left so that your weight gradually shifts from the inside of your right foot to the inside of your left foot.

This simple to-and-fro working of the ankles will, in itself, give supple golfers all the body motion they need while swinging. In fact, I teach a drill to junior golfers in which they never lift the left heel during the backswing, which deepens their sense of balance and forces them to develop a full arm swing. To provide a full body turn, older and less supple golfers may need to allow the left heel to lift slightly as they roll the ankle to the inside during the backswing. As far as the right heel is concerned, it should lift gradually as your arms swing forward and upward after impact. Basically, however, proper footwork is merely a matter of rolling the ankles as I've described.

"I put in many, many hours of exercises—like rocking sideways on my ankles—designed to teach me to stay on the inside of my right foot going back and the inside of my left coming down. . . . I must have played golf for three or four years before Jack Grout permitted me to raise my heels at all, (but) the dividends I've since reaped make me eternally

grateful to him for verbally whipping me into performing what was then a very boring regimen."—
JACK NICKLAUS

FUNDAMENTAL 5: *Full Extension*

"Achieving the widest possible arc has been a fundamental of my game since Jack Grout drummed its importance deep into my soul more than 20 years ago."—JACK NICKLAUS

Full extension is simply a matter of using all of your physical self as you swing—of fully stretching and coiling all the muscles of your body that need stretching and coiling. Most of that stretching and coiling is done during your backswing, to allow for later unstretching and uncoiling as you return the club back to the ball.

The comparison between full extension in the golf swing and full stretching of a bowstring in archery has been used before, but it remains useful in explaining a major purpose of the backswing. The tighter you pull the bowstring, the farther you'll shoot the arrow. In exactly the same way, the more you stretch and coil during your backswing, the greater your chances for creating high clubhead speed and thus of hitting the ball a long way.

FULL EXTENSION *on the backswing is required to hit your shots maximum distance. To achieve full extension you must (1) make as full a hip turn as you can without straightening your right leg or shifting weight onto the outside of that foot, (2) make as full a shoulder turn as you can without moving your head and (3) swing your hands as wide and as high as you can without shifting your head or loosening your grip.*

"If I hit the ball farther than most people, it isn't because I am stronger physically than they are, but because it became second nature for me at a young age to be fully extended muscularly as I performed the golf swing."—JACK NICKLAUS

Full extension is simple to explain, but physically demanding to execute. It involves doing three things during your backswing:

1. Making as full a turning of the hips as you possibly can, short of straightening your right leg or shifting weight onto the outside of your right foot.

2. Making as full a shoulder turn as you can while keeping your head steady.

3. Swinging your hands on as wide and as high an arc as you can, short of shifting your head position or loosening your hold on the club.

"I want my hands to go as high as possible. I like to have the feeling, as I near the top of the backswing, of trying to thrust them through the clouds. I just cannot get them too high."—JACK NICKLAUS

Full extension will give your golf swing maximum power, without forcing upon you the risk of inconsistency that results from extreme wristiness.

Full extension gives you the power you need to hit both high *and* low shots, instead of just low shots.

Full extension, because it requires a relatively slow backswing, improves your ability to make a well-timed forward swing.

Full extension makes it easier to resist the swing-shortening tautness that strikes all golfers to some extent as they get older. It conditions your body to play better golf longer.

FUNDAMENTAL 6: *Quiet Hands*

"The change of direction—it must be gentle."—
JACK NICKLAUS

Once you can apply the fundamentals of proper setup, grip, steady head, footwork, and full extension, there is really only one thing left that could spoil your overall golf swing. That would be "flashing" the club from the top of your backswing with your hands and wrists.

I suppose that it is only natural that we rely on our hands and wrists in golf, just as we use them for so many different functions in everyday living. I also suppose it is only natural that we tend to overuse our hands and wrists at the very start of our downswing, because it is at this time that our eagerness, or our anxiety, about striking the ball is most likely to overwhelm us.

"QUIET" HANDS *at the start of the downswing help preserve clubhead speed and keep the club moving on a proper path. The normal tendency of many golfers to "flash" or flip their hands and wrists too soon can be avoided through proper footwork and free swinging of the arms, while maintaining wrist cocking until near impact. In the drawings the increase of distance between the hands and the shoulders indicates free arm-swinging as opposed to shoving with the shoulders. Weight shifts from inside the right foot onto the left foot. However, the angle formed by the left arm and clubshaft, which indicates degree of wrist cock, remains intact.*

"Given a ghost of a chance, almost every golfer's hands will start to flash the club down to the ball way before any other part of his anatomy can go to work."—JACK NICKLAUS

Too much wristiness at the start of the downswing can ruin an otherwise superior golf swing, in that flashing the club down with the hands will either: (a) throw the clubhead off path, or (b) misalign the clubface, or (c) waste clubhead speed prior to impact, or (d) cause any combination of the above.

Like most young golfers who relish trying to bash the ball into the next country, Jack Nicklaus had the problem of flashing hands from almost the start of his days in golf. He finally mastered the problem and learned to keep his hands passive early in his downswing, but it took literally years of conscious effort and relentless physical practice.

"That was the hardest thing of all for me to do. . . . My method of keeping these limelight-hoggers (hands) backstage is to try to feel that they are not moving any faster on the first half of the forward swing than they did during the final phase of the backswing. When I'm successful, my shots fly farther because proper pace and sequence of down-

1 0 3

swing movement accelerate the club to maximum velocity at impact."—JACK NICKLAUS

The proper first move of the downswing involves the fundamental of footwork already mentioned—a lateral shifting of weight from the *inside* of the right foot to the *inside* of the left.

If you make this move *before* you start uncoiling your shoulders or uncocking your wrists, you will not only start your club down on a proper path, but you also may actually *increase* the extension and coiling of your muscles. This occurs because your feet and legs are shifting forward while your hands and club are still moving toward the finish of your backswing.

Once you develop your footwork as described in fundamental 4, this first move of the downswing will take place automatically, *so long as you give it time to happen*. While I don't believe that there should be an actual pause at the top of the backswing—some part of you should always be in motion—I do think that most golfers need to at least *feel* a momentary "waiting" at the top: a waiting with the hands and shoulders for the feet to shift some weight toward the target.

It is also extremely important that you remember always to *swing* the club. That may sound ridiculously elementary, but too many golfers, in their efforts to use their legs correctly, lose sight of the fact that it is the golf club that strikes the ball. While the feet start the downswing, the arms—not the hands—must do their part to swing the club down and forward and "through" the ball.

So long as your feet work correctly and lead your downswing, on all of your full shots you should try to accelerate your arms—and thus the club—through impact as fast as you possibly can without losing your balance. Do this and your hands will react automatically to the weight and speed of the moving clubhead. Do this and your wrists will uncock automatically to square the clubface at the proper time, so long as you also shift your weight and keep a steady head. You'll risk big trouble, however, if you consciously attempt to apply your hands and wrists to the shot.

ADVICE TO JUNIORS

At this point in your life, you have inside of you a God-given knack for imitating others. Use this knack by watching good golfers swing. As you do, keep in mind the six fundamentals I've described in this chapter. Watch how the experts apply them and the rhythm with which they apply them. The more you watch others act out the basics I've described, the easier it will be for you to master them yourself.

CHAPTER FIVE

Saving Shots

IN YOUR WAR AGAINST the golf course, the swing fundamentals from the last chapter—proper setup, grip, head position, footwork, extension, and "quiet" hands—represent the basic artillery you'll try to use on every normal full swing.

At times, however, your artillery will misfire. Or, even if you get to a point where you can execute the fundamentals perfectly, you can make a mental error or run into bad luck.

For instance, you might misjudge the length of an approach shot, choose the wrong club, and finish in a bunker short of the green, even though you made a perfect stroke. Or you may choose the right club, again make a perfect swing, and then watch with dismay as a sudden, unexpected gust of wind carries your shot over the green and into the tall grass beyond.

When your shots miss their mark, it really doesn't matter if you made a bad swing, used bad judgement, or simply suffered some bad luck. The scorecard only tells what you shot, not how you shot it. And, what's more, you'll soon discover that few, if any, of your friends really give a hoot about *how* you won or lost the war.

In golf, the score is the thing that matters—the *only* thing. Therefore, when your drive from the tee finishes behind a tree, or when you miss a green and your ball buries in sand, your mission for the moment becomes primarily to cut your losses—to save strokes—so that you can go on to the next hole with some chance of still winning the war.

In this chapter I will tell you how to plan and play the shots that you will most frequently need to fall back on when the battle goes against you. You will find, too, that many times these same stroke-saving shots, played in an effort to merely minimize your losses, will actually turn the battle, or even the war, in your favor. Many a match that seemed hopelessly lost has been won with a single, well-played "trouble" shot by a struggling golfer who refused to wave the white flag.

"Ask yourself this question: when you get in trouble, either through your own fault or through a bad break, which mental attitude will serve you best: infuriation and self-pity, or a philosophical and positive approach? I see a lot of bad temper and self-pity on tour, especially on difficult courses. I've been guilty of it myself at times. It's a human enough reaction. But even if anger or self-pity are excusable, I still dislike them intensely, in myself even more than in others. The reason is that they are crutches—copouts. You face a situation that you cannot cope with, so you give yourself an excuse for possible failure by getting mad at the course or the injustice you've suffered. The result invariably is that you fail to recover, not only from the one poor swing or unlucky bounce that first upset you, but from all the others that inevitably follow."—JACK NICKLAUS

CLUB SELECTION

Club selection applies to any discussion about saving strokes, because it is choosing the wrong weapon that often puts a player in trouble in the first place.

For example, if you were to pick almost any green on any course in the world, and were to stand by that green and watch the shots coming up to it, you'd find that the vast majority—at least 75 percent—finished *short* of the flagstick. And most of the remaining 25 percent would end up well past the hole. Only a handful out of every 100 approach shots would finish about "hole high."

Every club in your bag is designed to hit shots a different distance. The trick in club selection, therefore, is: (a) knowing your normal length of shot with each club, (b) knowing the length of the shot at hand, and (c) matching the two.

The simplest way to determine how far you can hit the ball with each club is simply to pace off the length of your shots. But first you must learn to take steps that are one yard in length. You can develop this skill in a matter of minutes by merely taking your yardstick, measuring off five yards of turf or flooring, and pacing that distance in five equal steps.

Thereafter, make it a habit to pace off the length of your good shots with various clubs, but only when the ball has carried and rolled a normal distance. Over a period of time, you will develop a precise knowledge of which club you should select and how hard you should swing it to make a shot of, say, 143 yards, or 167 yards, or 110 yards. You won't, of course, hit your shots the exact correct distance every time, or even most of the time, but you *will* come closer more often if you develop this awareness of what you and your clubs can actually do.

Once you have this awareness, judging distance at your "home"

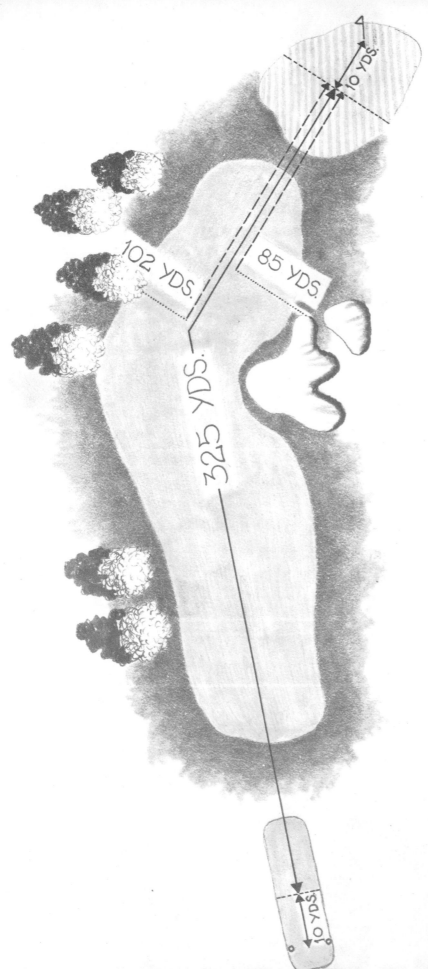

PROPER CLUB SELECTION for a given shot requires knowing how far you normally hit shots with each club, knowing the length of the shot at hand and matching the two pieces of information. Golf holes are measured from the center of the tee to the center of the green along the line of play intended by the course architect. The hole shown here, a dogleg to the right, is normally 325 yards. When the tee markers and flagstick are both positioned to the back, however, it would play an extra 20 yards in length. A golfer who normally drives 200 yards would need to plan on an approach shot of 145 yards instead of 125 yards, a difference of perhaps two or three clubs—a 6 or 7 iron, say, instead of a 9 iron. Some scorecards show the distance from a given object—a tree or a bunker, for example—to the center of the green. Again, however, this distance must be increased or decreased if the flagstick is back or forward of the center of the green.

course should never be a problem. This assumes, of course, that you have taken the time to pace off the distances to the center of each green from various spots along the way—from certain trees, bushes, sand traps, water sprinkler heads, and the like.

On "foreign" courses, determining yardage to the flagstick is still relatively easy. Bear in mind that holes are measured in yards from the middle of the tee to the middle of the green as the hole was designed for normal play. You will need first to note the yardage on the scorecard and then modify it according to the current positioning of the tee markers and the flagstick. On a big green, a flagstick set into the extreme front or back portion can subtract or add as many as 20–25 yards in "playing length" to the yardage listed on the scorecard.

Once you know a hole's playing length, it becomes relatively easy to determine how far your approach shot to the green must travel, by merely subtracting the total length of the shots you've already played from the hole's overall playing length.

On some courses you will find markers or bushes planted a given distance, usually 150 yards, from the center of the greens. Use these markers in your distance calculations on strange courses, but remember to modify the prescribed distance by the number of yards that the flagstick appears to be forward or back of the center of the green.

Most courses today are measured fairly reliably, but you will find some that give misleading yardages on the scorecard. Such badly-measured courses will become apparent to you after only a few holes. Thereafter, you'll need to rely on your sense of depth perception and your observation of the approach shots of others in your group. When in doubt about which of two clubs to use, note the hazards around the green. You'll probably want to use the longer club if the major trouble is in front of the green, or a shorter club if the maximum danger is behind it.

SHOT VISUALIZATION

Apart from applying the fundamentals of the previous chapter, and also selecting the right club, there is one other very important stroke-saving aid that you should apply on *every* shot you ever play. That one thing is simply to visualize the shot you intend to play *before* you play it. "See" the shot in your mind's eye—see it flying through the air and bouncing and rolling to the hole. Similarly, once you're on the green, visualize your putt rolling forward, perhaps curving somewhat with the slope of the green, and then nosediving into the cup.

The reason for this preshot visualization is simply to give your mind and your body a definite and positive course of action. Visualizing the shot before you swing is like visualizing a house that you've visited many times before. By visualizing it before you return to it, you can then drive to it quickly and surely without hesitation. By visualizing the golf shot beforehand, you tell your mind and body exactly what you expect them to accomplish, which encourages them to react accordingly by giving them a clear objective.

If you fail to flash a positive picture through your mind before swinging, you will often make an uncontrolled, undirected swing; or will swing with the same hesitancy you would use in driving to a house you'd never seen before in a neighborhood you'd never visited, slowing down here and there to check street signs and mail boxes for clues to where you are. If you flash a negative picture through your mind—say that of your shot curving into a pond—your mind and your body will tend to produce that particular bad shot unless you are able to redirect them at the last split second.

While proper preswing visualization will not guarantee a good shot every time, it *will* considerably increase your chances of success. It will aid you, too, in selecting the right club. And, while swinging, this visualization can help your mind and body to correct instinctively any errors you might have made in gripping, aiming, and setting up.

HILLY LIES

On shots where you are not actually shooting for the green itself, your target should almost always be a spot that is: (a) on the fairway, (b) on level ground, (c) well away from trouble, and that (d) allows you a clear shot to your next target.

Please reread that particular sentence, because it summarizes in a nutshell exactly what "position golf"—stroke-saving golf—is all about.

Inevitably, there will be times when your ball does not finish on level ground. In these cases, you will save yourself some strokes if you know beforehand how the ball reacts when struck from various types of angled lies.

Whenever the shot is a SIDEHILLER, with the ball either above or below your feet, you can expect that it will tend to fly *away from the slope of the hill*. Thus a shot with the ball above your feet will tend to PULL to the left of your target—away from the hillside—so aim to the right of your target initially. Conversely, when the ball is below your feet, aim the club and yourself more to the left of the target to allow for the ball's PUSHING out to the right—again, away from the hillside.

The ball will tend to PUSH to the right on DOWNHILL shots, so remember the phrase, "push down." Shots normally PULL to the left on UPHILL lies. Remember the phrase "pull up." Again, aim the club and yourself to offset the ball's anticipated reaction.

While it is important to aim properly on hilly lies, it is equally im-

HILLY LIES *require special adjustments; first, to help you maintain balance as you swing; second to offset the abnormal flight of the ball caused by the slope. All adjustments, however, can be made before you swing. When the ball is below your feet (far-left drawing) you should allow for it to push to the right by aiming your clubhead and yourself to the left. Hold the club at the end of the grip and keep your knees flexed so you can reach the ball. Keep your weight toward your heels to avoid falling forward. On shots with the ball above your feet (second drawing from left) the opposite procedure is needed. Plan for the ball to pull to your left, choke down on the grip, and keep your weight toward your toes. Remember that on sidehill lies the ball will generally tend to fly away from the hillside. On uphill and downhill lies (drawings on the right) set your body vertical to the slant of the slope with your weight on your high foot. Play the ball back in your stance on downhill lies to avoid catching the hill before your clubhead reaches the ball. Allow for uphill lies to pull to the left—remember "pull-up"— and for downhill lies to push to the right—remember "push-down."*

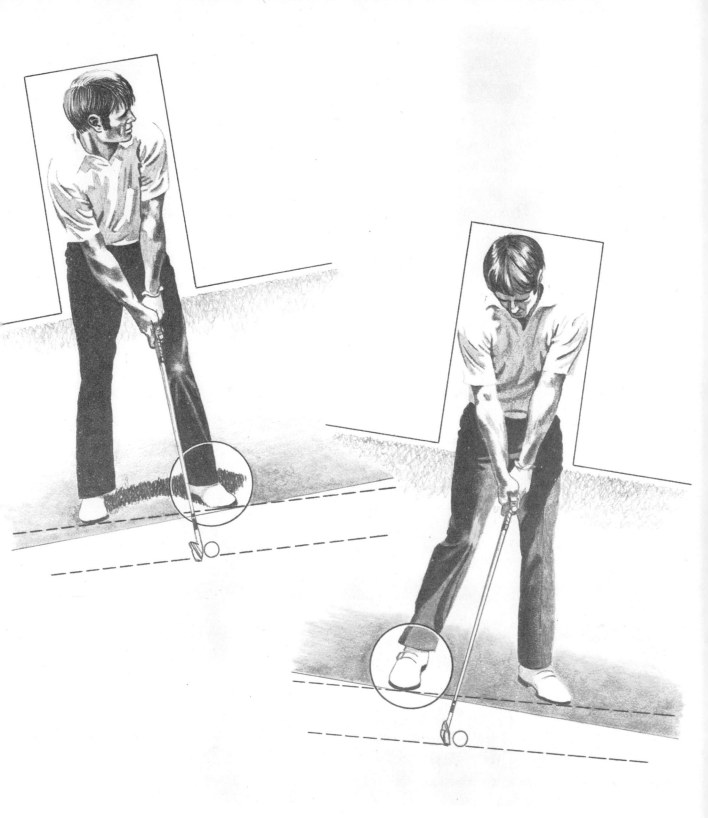

portant to maintain balance as you swing. The natural tendency will be to fall toward your downhill side, thus you must set your weight more toward your uphill foot at address, to brace yourself against the tendency. For the same reason, on sidehill lies set your weight more than normally toward your toes or heels, whichever are higher on the hill.

Having aimed correctly to offset pulling or pushing, and having set your weight to avoid falling down the hill, the only other thing you must do on hilly lies is to position yourself properly to make solid contact with the ball. On uphill and downhill lies this means tilting yourself to the right or left so that your whole body sets more or less perpendicular to the slope. This positions you to swing the clubhead *along* the slope instead of *into* it. You'll also find that, on downhill lies, you will make much better contact if you play the ball a bit more toward your high foot.

On sidehill lies when the ball is above your feet, and thus closer to your hands than normal, you must choke down on the club to avoid cutting under the ball. When it's below your feet—farther from your hands—you'll need to grip at the end of the club and stand a bit closer to the ball than normal to avoid topping the shot.

SHOTS FROM ROUGH

Your first and foremost thoughts on shots from long grass should be to play the type of shot that will let you hit your next one from short grass. Don't throw away the whole war in just one battle by slashing from rough to rough on shot after shot.

The next most important thought on shots from rough is choosing the correct club. The common tendency is to select an iron club with relatively little loft—say a 2, 3, or 4 iron—in hopes of regaining lost distance. These clubs demand an excellent lie with the ball sitting up cleanly on the grass. Without such a lie they lack sufficient loft to carry the ball out and over the deep surrounding grass, and lack sufficient clubhead weight to penetrate the heavy grass easily.

When in doubt between two clubs on a shot from deep rough, go with the one that has the most loft. Since the ball will then come out higher and cleaner, it will carry farther, which means that you'll lose very little if any distance.

The higher-lofted wood clubs—4, 5, and 6 woods—are handy weapons to use from fairly good lies when the grass isn't too deep or too thick, in that the beveled, wider bottoms of their heads tend to pancake the grass and slide over it readily. Thus they run into less resistance from the grass than do the thin-bladed irons.

Finally, the best technique to use from rough is one that reduces the amount of grass that might intervene between your clubhead and the ball. Here particularly is where an upright swing is better than a flat swing, because the clubhead moves down to the ball at a sharper angle, which allows less grass to slow down the clubhead's speed. Playing the ball an inch or two further back in your stance—toward your right foot—is the simplest and surest way to steepen your clubhead's angle of attack, so long as you maintain a steady head as you swing.

When the deep grass lays toward you—away from your target—always figure on it slowing down your clubhead and turning it to the left of your target through impact. So aim to the right and use more club (less loft). When the grass runs from your ball to the target, use less club, because the ball will tend to carry slightly less backspin and, as a result, will dart and roll forward faster and farther than is usual.

"PART-SHOTS"—CHIPPING AND PITCHING

There will be times during every round you play when a full shot with even a 9 iron or a wedge would overshoot your target. Then you need to

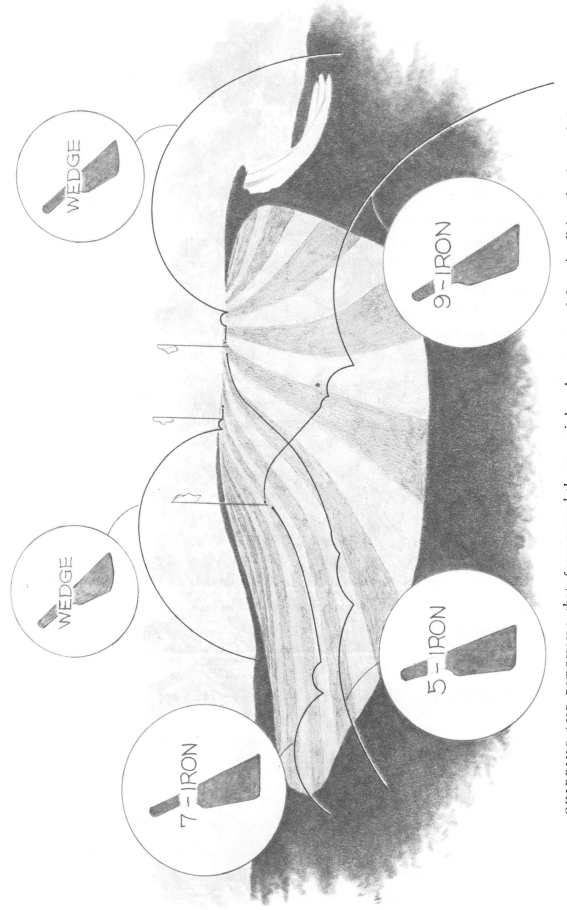

CHIPPING AND PITCHING shots from around the green is largely a matter of first visualizing the shot and then choosing the club most likely to reproduce it. Whenever possible plan shots that will land on a level portion of the green. Also, plan shots that bounce and roll, rather than carry, to the hole whenever they seem possible to play without the ball running well beyond the flagstick. The drawing shows various shot situations you will encounter and the ideal way to play them. The clubs shown for each are suggested types. With practice and experience you may find that different clubs are better for you.

know how to play "part-shots"—strokes made with less than a full swing. I discuss part-shots in this chapter because, more often than not, you'll find yourself playing them after you've messed up a full shot, when you need a good recovery to save a stroke or two.

There are two basic types of part-shots—"chip" shots and "pitch" shots. When you play them you are either "chipping" or "pitching."

The main difference between a chip shot and a pitch shot is their trajectory. Your basic chip shot features minimum "carry" and maximum roll, ideally landing just on the green and bouncing and rolling the rest of the way to the hole. The basic pitch shot features maximum carry and minimum roll, landing close to the hole and then, hopefully, stopping with little additional forward movement.

Both of these part-shots are essential to every golfer's shotmaking arsenal. The higher pitch shot is usually the more risky of the two in that, to fly the ball high and settle it quickly, it must be played with a highly-lofted club—one of the wedges or the 9 iron. Thus it takes a longer swing to pitch the ball the same distance you could chip it with a less-lofted club, and for most golfers the longer swing increases the risk of mishitting the ball.

The variety of part-shot situations you'll encounter during a single golf season is practically endless. For example, a ball that sets low in the grass will react differently from a ball that sets up high, while certain types of grasses on greens will "grab" a pitch shot quicker than will other types. However, in time and with experience, you'll learn to sense and anticipate how a given chip or pitch shot will react, and how it should be played for the best results. For the moment, you'll be a far better chipper and pitcher immediately if you follow these suggestions:

1. Always visualize how you *think* the shot should look before you play it.

2. Visualize a part-shot landing on the green whenever conditions

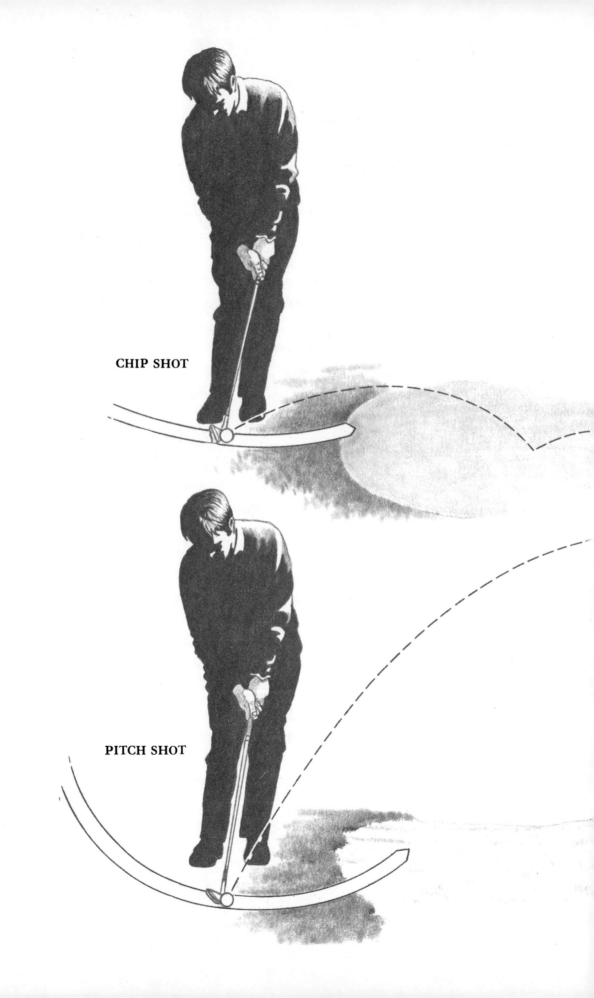

CHIP SHOT

PITCH SHOT

CHIP SHOTS *(shown in upper drawing) are low flying and long running because a less lofted club is used and because the clubhead path is relatively shallow back and through.* PITCH SHOTS *(lower drawing) fly high and settle quickly upon landing. They require a more lofted club and a steeper clubhead path. Such a path results from using more wrist cocking and uncocking than on chip shots. In both cases, however, your hands should slightly lead the clubhead through impact so that contact is made just BEFORE the clubhead reaches the bottom of its arc, when it is still moving somewhat downward. Attempts to scoop the ball into the air generally fail. The clubhead either cuts into the ground behind or under the ball or, more often, flips upward into the back or top of it, causing a low, driving shot that goes too far.*

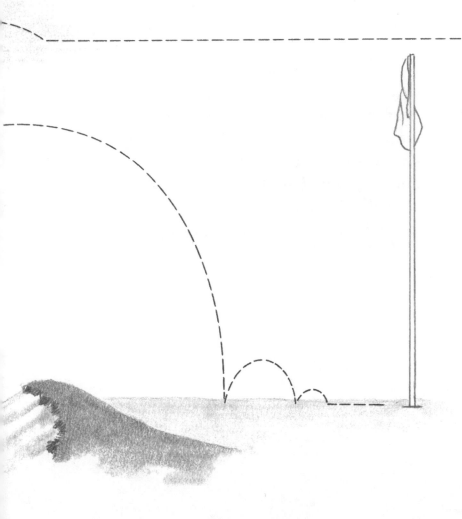

allow, because it's surface is smoother and more consistent than the fairway.

3. Visualize a part-shot landing on a level area of the green whenever possible.

4. Whenever possible, visualize a chip shot rather than a pitch shot. "See" the ball landing five or six feet onto the green and then rolling to the hole. Pitch the ball to the hole only when running the chip shot would make the ball roll well past the cup, or when chipping would force you to land the ball on a hillside.

5. Choose the club that will most easily give you the shot you've visualized.

6. Take one or more practice swings until you find the stroke you will need to produce the shot you've visualized with the club you've chosen.

7. Duplicate the stroke you've rehearsed as you make your actual shot.

When practicing chipping and pitching, here are the basics of technique that you should try to master:

1. The shorter the shot, the more you should choke down on the club, narrow your stance, and stand closer to the ball. In effect, give yourself maximum control of the clubhead by gripping closer to it, short of actually holding onto the metal part of the shaft.

2. Try to catch the ball at the bottom, or just *before* the bottom, of your swing arc. Strike it with a *downward*-forward action of the clubhead, never with an *upward*-forward scoop. On chip shots use a shallower swing arc—more forward than downward. On pitch shots use a steeper arc—more downward than forward. These different arcs make your chip shots run forward and your pitch shots pop upward.

3. Make sure your left hand leads, not follows, your clubhead through impact, to help assure that the clubhead moves downward, not upward, to the ball.

4. Make sure your forearms accelerate, not decelerate, through impact, to avoid flipping the clubhead upward with your hands.

5. Keep your head very steady.

SAND SHOTS

Even experienced golfers sometimes tremble a bit when faced with the need to save strokes from sand. I suppose this insecurity is normal when you consider that the basic sand shot is the only stroke in golf where the clubhead doesn't actually touch the ball, but rather cuts under it through a relatively unfamiliar substance. However, I think you'll find sand shots much simpler to play with less worry if you will follow the style I learned over a quarter century ago from my good friend Sidney Saloman, Jr., former part-owner of the St. Louis baseball teams and currently owner of the St. Louis Blues hockey club.

The first thing you need to play these shots well is a sand wedge, a club that is specially designed for bunker play in that its head is heavy enough to cut readily under the ball and through the sand, yet is built in a way that keeps it from cutting too deeply. If you were to hold the head of a sand wedge at eye level in front of you, with the shaft vertical, you would see that its bottom, or sole, differs from that of all other clubs in that the sole's leading edge is actually *higher* than its trailing edge.

The lower back edge of the sole is called the "bounce" of the club. When properly applied to the sand, it acts as a rudder to keep the clubhead from cutting too deeply, and thus slowing down so much that the ball doesn't even clear the edge of the bunker. Once you learn to use the bounce on your sand wedge, you need not fear sloshing around in the sand, shot after shot, any more. You will see how the bounce works if you set the sand wedge on a level surface and gradually turn the clubface open to the right. You'll notice that the leading edge gradually raises until

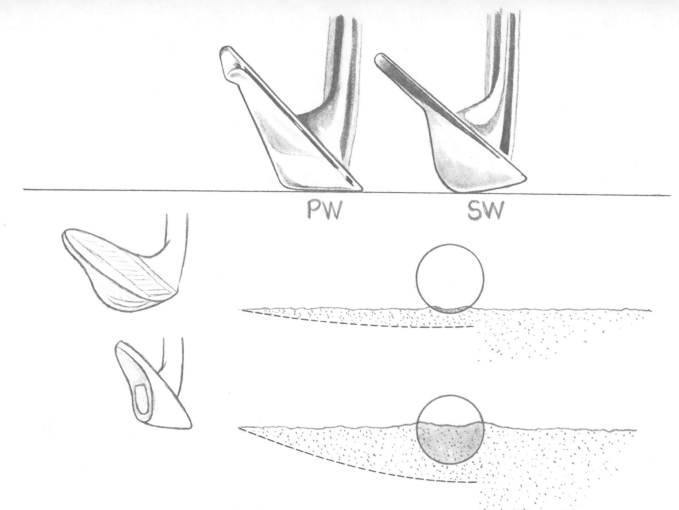

ON NORMAL SAND SHOTS, *the clubhead should slide under the ball so that the ball flies out on a "cushion" of sand. Your success in sand depends largely on consistently producing the correct cushion for the shot at hand. Once you learn to take the proper cut of sand every time, you can control the distance your ball will fly by merely regulating the force of your swing. The drawings show what you must do to make the correct cut of sand time after time.*

First, note the difference in the construction of the sand wedge (SW) and pitching wedge (PW). The bottom, or "sole," of the pitching wedge angles downward, with the leading edge lower than the trailing edge. The sole of the sand wedge, however, angles slightly upward, with the trailing edge lower than the leading edge. The lower trailing edge of the sand wedge—its "bounce"—can be used as a rudder to keep the clubhead from knifing too far into the sand. The more you open your clubface to the right at address, the lower the rudder sets, the shallower will be the cut of sand it takes. The more you close it to the left at address, the more the leading edge turns downward, the deeper will be your cut of sand. In short, when you have a shallow lie in the sand, open your clubface to the right at address for a shallow cut under the ball. Close it to the left when you need a deeper cut to slide under a buried lie.

Next, after setting your clubface for the proper depth of cut, cock your wrists early in your backswing. This gives you a steep backswing which, in turn, allows for a steep downswing. The steep downswing helps assure that your clubhead will indeed slide down and under the ball, and not bounce forward off the sand and into the back of it.

Finally, as you swing down and forward, try to use the same footwork as on normal shots, with your legs sliding forward. This foot and leg work shifts your weight onto your left foot and adds length to your cut of sand. The longer the cut of sand you can make, the farther behind the ball you can make your point of entry and still slide under it. A normal 10-to 12-inch slice of sand allows you to enter a good four inches behind the ball, a safe distance to avoid contacting the ball itself.

the club actually rests on its bounce. Then, as you gradually turn the face back to the left, the sharper leading edge turns gradually downward.

You can control the depth of your cut in the sand by the openness or closedness of the clubface as you address the ball. The more you open the clubface to the right, the more you'll apply the club's bounce effect as you swing through the sand, and the shallower will be your slice of sand. The more you close your clubface at address, the more you'll use its leading edge and the deeper it will penetrate the sand.

Thus, the deeper your ball sits in the sand, the less you'll want to open your clubface at address. When most of the ball is lower than the surrounding level of the sand, you'll need to start with your clubface actually closed to the left of the target. Remember, the goal is to cut *under* the ball without cutting so deeply that your clubhead can't move readily through the sand.

Naturally, you'll find that the ball flies and rolls to the left of your target when you close your clubface in that direction, and to the right of target when you open it to the right. To counteract this misdirection, merely align *yourself*—especially your shoulders—more right of target when you close the clubface, and more left of target when you open it.

While clubface alignment controls the depth of your sand "divot," so to a somewhat lesser degree does your angle of attack. In bunkers you want a fairly steep clubhead approach to the sand so that it is sure to cut *under* the ball, instead of merely slapping the surface like a pebble on water and bouncing up into the ball's back side. In short, you must steepen your angle of attack in sand to assure cutting under the ball, but use enough of the club's bounce to avoid cutting too deeply.

To give your swing this steepness, use an early wrist cock on your backswing to get the clubhead moving abruptly upward. Then apply a strong, downward pulling action with your left hand and arm on your downswing.

Finally, use your legs as much as you can during your forward swing. Dig yourself into the sand at address and then work your ankles as best you can, as I described in the previous chapter. The more you can use your legs on your forward swing, the longer the slice of sand you will take, and the longer the slice you can take, the farther behind the ball you can enter the sand without fear of bouncing the clubhead into its back side.

With practice, most golfers can take at least a 12-inch slice of sand without difficulty. Thus they can cut into the sand a good four or five inches behind the ball. This all but eliminates the so-called "thin" shot, the one that catches only the ball—no sand—at full clubhead speed and airmails it over the green.

Normal sand shot technique thus becomes nothing more than:

1. Opening or closing your clubface to apply the correct amount of bounce to produce the correct depth of divot to cut beneath the bottom of the ball.

2. Aligning yourself to offset for the openness or closedness of your clubface, so that your ball will fly toward your target.

3. Cocking your wrists early in your backswing and then pulling the club *downward* to the sand, well behind and then under the ball.

4. Shifting your weight onto your left foot early in your down-swing, to assure a long enough slice of sand.

5. Keeping your head steady throughout your swing.

If you follow this method, you can make approximately the same swing on every normal sand shot you play. Only its force needs to vary, to determine the length of the shot.

This technique also applies in all types of sand—wet or dry, coarse or powdery. The only variation you'll need to make is in the amount of bounce you apply. Since wet or coarse sand resists clubhead penetration, you'll need less bounce and more leading edge to cut under the ball.

Therefore address the ball with the clubface less open, or more closed, than normal.

Extremely dry or soft sand, especially the powdery type, affords less resistance to the moving clubhead, which therefore tends to cut too deeply and decelerate too fast unless you apply more bounce and less leading edge. So, in dry or soft sand, address the ball with a more open clubface than normal.

Find out how far you can make the ball fly when you use this method on a full-force swing. Then, whenever you run into a sand shot that is longer than your maximum, you'll need to change your technique slightly. You'll need to make absolutely sure that your clubhead contacts the ball *before* it enters the sand.

To assure such contact, merely play the ball far enough back in your stance (to your right) so that you can "trap" it near the end of your downswing, *before* your clubhead path becomes level or starts upward. Also, be sure to dig your feet in solidly to avoid slippage, and to shorten your grip on the club, again to make certain that you avoid catching any sand behind the ball.

Because you play the ball farther back in your stance on this shot, your clubface will carry less loft than normal at impact, causing the ball to fly lower than normal for the club you have in hand. Therefore, be sure you select a club with more than enough loft to assure that your ball will clear the lip of the bunker.

And, above all, remember that sand traps are *hazards*. That being so, you cannot "ground" your clubhead or otherwise touch the sand with your club until you swing it forward during your actual stroke. The penalty for breaking this rule is two strokes in stroke play or loss of the hole in match play.

PUTTING

In the end, after you've escaped from trouble, your final effort to conserve shots will take place on the putting green. A putt that hangs on the lip of the hole and then finally topples in can offset fully a penalty stroke for flubbing a shot into a lake or stream. But when that same putt fails to drop, the effect on your score is exactly the same as if you'd completely muffed a tee shot.

For this reason, putting is the ultimate strokesaver. And, since the object of golf is to take the fewest possible strokes, doesn't it make sense that golfers should devote considerable time to putting practice? I should think so, but few golfers really do practice putting; most seem to prefer banging away at tee shots. Those players who compete at golf for a living spend more time working on their putting than on any other type of shot, and I suggest that you follow their example if you really want to become good at the game.

Good putting is primarily a matter of confidence, planning, sensitivity, and sound technique. All these ingredients are important, but if I could have a full measure of only one, I'd certainly choose confidence. If you *know* you are going to hole a certain putt, you can all but stand on your head and the ball will still find the cup.

"Confidence has to be the golfer's greatest single weapon on the greens. If he believes he can get the ball into the hole, a lot of the time he will, even if

his techniques appear unorthodox or even down-right faulty. If he doesn't believe he can get the ball into the hole, most of the time he won't, even though his technique may seem flawless."—JACK NICKLAUS

———————————————————————

Unfortunately, confidence isn't something you can buy at the pro shop. It comes, in part, from knowing that you've planned your putt—"read the green"—correctly. It comes further from sensing in your hands that you can produce the putt you've planned. And it comes finally from applying a technique that does, in fact, produce the putt you've planned.

In short, while confidence in putting is more important even than planning, sensitivity, and sound technique, it actually derives from these three ingredients.

And all three require two things—practice and practical experience. The more putts you plan and stroke, both on the practice green and under pressure on the course, the greater will be your ability to read greens, sense distance and direction, and actually strike the ball as you've planned and sensed that it should be struck.

Planning putts involves reading the character of terrain and grass between your ball and the hole. It means sensing just how fast the ball must run, and in which direction it must curve, if any, to finish in the hole. In the end, before you putt, you should clearly "see" in your mind's eye the ball rolling toward and into the cup. If you are a sensitive putter with a good putting stroke, "What you sees," as Flip Wilson says, "is what you gets."

Often there are several different ways to sink a given putt. Let's say you have a 5-foot sidehiller that obviously will curve from left to right.

The amount it will curve depends, really, on how firmly you strike the ball. The faster you make it travel, the less it will curve sideways. Thus you can tap it gently and let it curve as much as six to ten inches to the right, or you can ram it forward and expect only an inch or two of "break." Consequently, every putt requires two decisions—how firmly to strike the ball and where to aim it.

Once you've made these two decisions, once you can visualize the ball curving the amount you've decided upon at the speed you've anticipated, you should consciously carry this image in your mind's eye until after you've actually sent the putt on its way. The stronger the image you can retain of the putt's being successful, as you stroke it, the greater your chances are of actually holing it.

There are many tricks to reading greens correctly, and you will discover what works best for you as you practice and play the game. For the moment, however, here are a few observations you might wish to consider in planning putts:

1. The faster the ball will roll on the green, the less it will curve sideways.

2. A ball will roll fastest during the early stages of a putt, and thus will be more likely to curve sideways near the hole when it's slowing down.

3. Most greens—at least 95 percent—slant downward to some degree from back to front.

4. Sidehill putts are likely to curve more on greens with grass that is (a) dry, (b) cut short, and (c) sparse or thin-bladed, especially when the putt is moving slowly.

5. You can expect less sidehill break on greens with grass that is: (a) wet, (b) cut long and growing, (c) thick or thick-bladed.

Once you've read the putt and visualized it in your mind's eye, you can move from the planning stage to the sensing stage. Most of your sens-

GOOD PUTTING *requires that you apply your mind as well as your body, as Jack Nicklaus does in these drawings. First, look at the area over which your putt must travel and, in your mind's eye, "see" it rolling toward and into the hole along the path you feel it should take (see figure on the left). As you address the putt with your eyes over your intended line (middle figure), continue to "see" the putt you plan to make, but also sense in your hands and arms how it will feel to actually reproduce it. Finally, as you stroke your putt, accelerating your hands forward (drawing on right), continue to visualize the putt you are trying to make.*

ing is done in your fingers. Therefore, I suggest that you hold your putter as lightly as you can while still maintaining control. Keep this same slight grip pressure consistent throughout your putting stroke and avoid sudden grabbing.

Regarding the mechanics of good putting, I prefer to keep them to a minimum, largely because overconcern about mechanics can diminish your visualization of the putt's being successful and your sensitivity for executing it. Therefore, I will mention only those basic mechanics that I feel are mandatory for good putting. These are:

1. Be comfortable over the ball as you address the putt.

2. Set your head in a position so that your eyes are slightly behind— to the right of—the ball, but still on the path of your putt if it were extended through the ball. This allows you to use the ball as you would a gun sight when you aim the putterhead down the path along which you wish to swing it.

3. Keep your head steady as you putt.

4. Always accelerate your forearms through the contact area on your forward stroke, so that your hands won't take over and flip the clubface open or closed.

5. Again, hold the club lightly and keep a picture of the ball toppling into the hole in your mind's eye as you stroke.

Beyond these basics there is a great latitude for individualism in putting. Use whatever method you find works for you, so long as it allows you to *consistently* make *solid contact* with your putterhead moving down, not across, the line of the putt.

CHAPTER SIX

Getting Better

I'VE NEVER SEEN a youngster practice golf like Jack Nicklaus did. He'd come out to Scioto in the worst possible weather you could imagine —snow, rain, strong winds, extreme heat. During the summers he'd average about 300 practice shots a day in addition to playing 18 to 36 holes.

There were a few times, though, when I felt he was neglecting his golf. Usually, I'd merely mention this to his father, Charlie, and, sure enough, Jackie would show up the next day ready to go.

Once I happened to tell Bill Foley, a friend of mine and of Jack's who worked on the Columbus newspaper, that "Jackie's 15,000 to 20,000 balls behind in his practice." I didn't think anything more about what I'd said until the next morning. Then I saw my comment printed in the paper. That afternoon Jackie was on the practice tee firing away, and he was still there quite a while after it grew too dark to see the balls finish.

*"Jack Grout ALWAYS told me that. He STILL tells me that. 'Let's go, Jackie Buck,' he'd say. 'You're 15,000 to 20,000 balls behind, Jackie Buck.' "—*JACK NICKLAUS

This chapter is about improving your golfing skills, about developing and grooving your fundamentals. Certainly, proper practice habits play a big part in that effort. So too do face-to-face lessons and actual competitive experience. I'll talk about those things, but first I want to explain and forewarn about some things you can expect to happen to you when you get serious about improving your golf.

The first thing you should understand is that progress in golf comes in peaks and valleys. One day you'll peak; you'll shoot your "career" round. "Now I've got it," you'll say. "I've found the secret."

The next day, or shortly thereafter, you may play just about as dismally as you ever could imagine. Nothing will work. You'll find yourself in the valley of despair.

On these bad days, it's best to remember what I've said about progressing through peaks and valleys. If you continue to work on your fundamentals and your stroke-saving shots, you'll find that gradually your peaks will get higher and higher, and so will the bottoms of your valleys.

The second thing you should know about progress in golf is that sometimes you'll play your *worst* after you've been practicing and working very hard on something new. Our bodies are slaves to habit. They resist new positions and new movements. Changes usually feel foreign, often uncomfortable. This discomfort is usually temporary, but it can definitely cause you to hit bad shots and shoot high scores until the new technique starts feeling natural.

The point is: don't give up on a sound fundamental just because it doesn't work at first. You probably have been "grooving" your mistakes for some time. It may take considerable effort to rechannel your swing until it feels natural and comfortable. In the process you may find that new or unfamiliar sensations force you to unconsciously alter your swing rhythm, or inadvertently change your grip pressure—just two of the many things that can throw your game temporarily off stride. What I'm asking you to do is never to let a few bad shots sway you from mastering a valid fundamental.

"Sure I get discouraged. We all do. But you have to expect some bad shots. Don't change your whole swing unless the bad shots become chronic. You keep changing and changing everything and you'll never know where you are."—JACK NICKLAUS

A third discouraging thing that frustrates the vast majority of golfers as they try to improve is the difficulty they run into when they try to take their newfound skills from the practice tee to the golf course itself. Nothing is more likely to thwart a learning golfer than to hit shot after shot perfectly on the range, and then to dub one after another in his first try at shooting a good score.

When this happens—and it no doubt will, at times—instead of chucking it all in, remember these *facts:*

• On the practice tee, you hit shot after shot with the same club. On the course, you seldom use the same club twice in a row.

• On the practice tee, you hit shot after shot in rapid-fire succession. On the course, walking and waiting between shots, you allow time for muscles to tighten and for at least some of your sense of rhythm to dull.

• On the practice tee, you invariably hit shots from a level lie. On the course you frequently are required to hit from angled lies.

• On the practice tee, you need not fear incurring a penalty if you hit a shot off line. On the course, this danger is invariably present.

• On the practice tee, a bad shot costs you nothing but wasted motion. On the course, it could cost you a battle, or even the war.

All these things make playing golf much more difficult than practicing golf. And I hope that, by understanding why this is so, you'll keep forging ahead with your golf improvement program, even when it seems that you're getting worse instead of better.

TAKING LESSONS

I've tried to make this book a valid guide for both new golfers and more experienced players who wish to gain a new lease of golfing life. It covers the basics that one needs to play the game well. I would not want you to think, however, that it precludes individual, face-to-face instruction.

As golfers, we may think we understand the swing. We may feel we are swinging correctly. However, we cannot readily *see* ourselves swing. Therefore we occasionally need a professional observer to check us out, to note any mistakes, and to put us back on the right track.

Also, while a book can detail golfing fundamentals and impart considerable knowledge, it cannot tailor specific instruction to the fine degree you would need to become some day another Jack Nicklaus. To even approach that level of skill, you'll need personal attention from a teacher who can deal with your own personal physical and mental quirks.

I cannot teach you face to face, but I can tell you how to get maximum benefit when you do go to someone who can. I suggest that at that time you:

1. Realize beforehand that the teacher probably will not work a miracle with your game. He won't put a magic wand to your forehead and turn you into a par-shooter. In short, be ready to be patient. Delight in your good shots, but expect to hit some bad ones at first.

2. Explain to him your golfing goals, and tell him how much time and effort you can and will spend to reach them. He'll then know how to tailor his teaching to fit your aspirations and commitment.

3. Be open-minded. Remember, *you* are the learner, not the teacher.

4. Listen carefully. And channel your attention to your teacher's message, even when you're dying to start hitting shots. If your teacher is stressing grip, for instance, don't concern yourself about stance.

5. Ask questions when you don't understand any message. Don't hesitate to ask what, specifically, the instructional message is supposed to accomplish. With such information you'll gradually learn to relate a given action to a given result, and vice-versa.

6. Ask your pro for a priority list of the things you should practice, and the order in which you should tackle them.

7. Ask your pro what specific bad shots you will hit when you have failed to apply his message. By finding out what shots result from what specific mistakes, you can on your own later diagnose your failures by the types of shot they produce.

8. Book a follow-up lesson to: (a) correct any misapplication of the message that you might have made, and (b) to take additional instruction for moving on to the next step in your advancement.

9. Practice your given priorities astutely and resolutely between lessons.

Regarding point 8 above, I find that many pupils skip from teacher to teacher when they do not improve immediately. This isn't fair to the professional, but, more important, it keeps these pupils from developing consistency in their games. There will be times when a pro gives a bad lesson—we are all human—but far more often it is the pro's message that is sound and the public's execution that is weak. Usually, a follow-up lesson eliminates this problem and opens the way for future advancement.

ADVICE TO PARENTS

I'm often asked at what age should a child start golf lessons. It's difficult to answer this question specifically, because some children at 10 have the psychological awareness of a 15-year-old, and some 15-year-olds goof around like 10-year-olds. Jack Nicklaus was always about six years ahead of his actual age when it came to golf.

The best answer I can give to this question is that youngsters should not be pushed into lessons until they show an interest in learning the game, and until they have the attention span, concentration, and understanding that learning golf demands. Actually, I prefer to see youngsters start with group lessons, when they are about 10 or 11 years old. In group sessions they have more fun, gain inspiration from the success of others, and also learn from others' failures. Individual lessons can follow a year or two later.

If your child does take lessons, you should not attempt to instruct him in any way unless you have attended his previous lessons and totally understand the instruction he was given. Then your message should merely reinforce the pro's. Usually, any additional suggestions from you, however well-meant, will merely dilute the pro's advice and confuse your child.

"The best advice I could give parents would be to put their youngsters in good hands—not their own hands. That's about it. All I hope for my own kids

is that I can get them taught the fundamentals and keep their interest alive."—JACK NICKLAUS

PRACTICING

I cannot think of a single skill that we can't do better with practice. That goes for everything from laying bricks to whistling through your teeth. And golf is certainly no exception to that rule. In fact, golf demands constant practice merely to *maintain* one's level of skill.

All great golfers have been great practicers at some time or other in their lives. Unfortunately, all great practicers have not necessarily become great golfers, or even good ones.

There is much more to practicing than merely striking golf balls. Practicing golf is an art unto itself. The sooner you master that art, the better you'll play. The more you improve the quality of your practice, the less quantity you'll need.

"*A lot of players seem to practice by just going through the motions of waving the club in the air. When I practice I try to put the same care into every shot that I would if I were hitting it in a tournament.*"—JACK NICKLAUS

The following pieces of advice will help you get maximum benefit out of your practice sessions:

1. Isolate yourself as much as you can. Good practice demands your maximum concentration.

2. Always practice with a goal clearly in mind, whether it be to improve one of your fundamentals, increase your skill on a particular shot, develop a certain feeling in your swing, or whatever.

---

*"Even before a round, when you'd think I'm just loosening up, I'm really learning as I practice. The range may be 100 yards wide and I might be scattering balls from one side to the other. It might look like I'm hitting some absolutely horrible golf shots. But I'm really not. I'm experimenting to find out exactly what I can do that particular day. Then I won't be apt to try something on the course that I can't pull off."—*JACK NICKLAUS

---

3. Stick to your priorities, whether they've been set by you or by your instructor. Don't switch to a new swing thought every time you miss two or three shots in a row.

4. Select a target before every practice shot you play.

5. Visualize every practice shot before you play it.

6. Watch your shots fly through the air and land and roll. This is the only way to link a certain type of swing or a certain swing feeling with a specific result. The sooner you can link certain swings with certain

results, the sooner you'll be able actually to produce the shots you visualize before swinging.

7. When your shots are consistently worse than normal for a period of time—say for 20–30 shots in a row—check out your basic fundamentals, especially your grip, aim, and setup.

8. Practice your stroke-saver shots—shots from hilly lies, sand, part-shots, and putting.

9. Avoid practicing when you are tired, physically or mentally.

ADVICE TO PARENTS

I have found that many youngsters like to rebel. Tell them to play golf and they'll go swimming. Suggest they go swimming and they'll play golf.

I find this is less of a problem if the parent also works on his or her game while the child practices. Make your child's practice fun. Challenge him to hit shots straighter than you hit yours, for instance. Or offer a soft drink if he or she can put a sand shot within a club-length of the hole in, say, ten shots. Or tell him he needs to make 50 percent of his 12-foot putts before he can hope to win an imaginary U.S. Open.

Whatever you do, let your children know how pleased you are with their successes. Praise them for all good shots. Make golf a game that they enjoy excelling at.

COMPETITION

Jack Nicklaus shot a 51 for nine holes the first time he ever played golf. He was ten years old at the time. Three years later he won the Ohio State Junior Championship, competing against boys three and four years his senior. At 16 he beat the best professional golfers in Ohio, winning the state open title with final rounds of 64 and 72. At 19 he won the U.S. Amateur Championship, and at 21 he did it again. In between, he came within two shots of winner Arnold Palmer in the biggest tournament of all, the U.S. Open. Playing as a professional since 1962, Jack has dominated the game, finishing first, second, or third in over twice as many PGA tour events as any other competitor.

I'm sure that Jack would never have amassed such an impressive record without his tremendous desire to compete, and his father's willingness to sacrifice, financially and otherwise, to see that he had the opportunity to do so.

Competition, whether it be for the U.S. Open or a mere 50-cent nassau match, is the stimulant that all successful golfers relish. It's the spice that makes all the hours of practice worthwhile.

I suggest that you enter every tournament you can. Looking forward to a competition will encourage you to work harder at your game. It will give new meaning to the instruction you receive here, and from your own pro. It will add to your appreciation for the true depth of golf, as a many-sided challenge to your mind as well as to your body. It will give you the satisfaction of meeting and overcoming this challenge. It will show you new avenues for improvement. It will bring you into healthy contact and camaraderie with many fine people whom you might otherwise never meet. Also, it will teach you how to lose—and hopefully how to win—graciously.

As you compete in golf, there will be times when you'll find yourself extremely nervous. This should not shame or worry you because it is natural—even Jack Nicklaus gets nervous at times. There will be occasions when you will be embarrassed by your bad play, and this shouldn't overconcern you either, because Jack also embarrasses himself at times; but he accepts this embarrassment in the right vein—as a challenge to eliminate its cause.

I hope you will react the same way if your game goes sour. If it does, first reread chapter four of this book. Review the six fundamentals therein in light of your own play. I strongly suspect you'll find a clue to the cause of your poor or embarrassing play. In most cases, the cure will require little more than one or two simple, minor adjustments.

And, above all else, I hope you will never lose sight of the fact that golf is, indeed, a *game*. It's something to have fun doing. A good shot is something to watch and enjoy, to take a moment to savor. I sincerely hope that this book helps to give you many such moments during your life in golf.

WHAT GOLFERS SAY

Glossary of Terms

THE FOLLOWING IS a glossary of basic terminology. As in other chapters of this book, any definitions involving the words "clockwise" or "counterclockwise," and "right" and "left" in the directional or anatomical sense, are presented as they would apply to righthanded golfers.

ACE: Playing a hole in one stroke. Also a "hole-in-one."
ADDRESS: The position of the player at the ball before swinging.
ADDRESSING THE BALL: The act of placing oneself in position for swinging and—except when the ball is in a hazard—grounding the clubhead.
ADVICE: Any counsel or suggestion which could influence a player in determining his strategy, choice of club, or method of making a stroke.
AIR SHOT: See "whiff."
ANGLE OF ATTACK: Steepness of clubhead's path of approach to the ball on the forward swing.
APPROACH: A shot to a green not made from the teeing area. Also, the area in front of the green.
APRON: Grassy area immediately adjacent to a green, usually cut shorter than fairway grass but longer than the grass on the green itself.
AWAY: Designation for ball or its owner farthest from flagstick and thus next in turn to play.
BACK DOOR: Side of cup farthest from player.
BACK NINE: Second nine holes of an 18-hole course.
BACKSPIN: Reverse spin imparted to ball when struck.
BANANA BALL: Slang for a shot that curves from left to right.

BENT: A finely-textured species of grass.

BERMUDA: A coarsely-textured species of grass.

BEST-BALL: A match in which one golfer plays against the better ball of two players or the best ball of three players. (Term is commonly misapplied to "four-ball" matches).

BIRDIE: A score of one stroke under par on a hole.

BITE: Backspin sufficient to make ball stop quickly, or actually bounce and roll backwards, upon landing.

BLADE: To catch back side of ball with leading edge of iron club and cause a low, driving shot. Also describes a thin, metal-headed putter.

BLAST: Type of bunker shot in which clubhead displaces a relatively large amount of sand.

BLIND BOGEY: Competition in which player estimates before starting what handicap will be needed to put his net score between 70 and 80, and thus qualify him for a blind drawing of a winning number in that range.

BLIND HOLE: One on which green cannot be seen by player making a normal approach shot.

BLIND SHOT: Approach shot on which golfer cannot see the flagstick.

BOGEY: One stroke over par on a given hole. In Great Britain, sometimes used as the number of strokes a better-than-average golfer is expected to take on a hole.

BORROW: The amount a player allows for a putt to curve sideways on a slanted green.

BOUNCE: The extension below horizontal of a portion of a club's sole; usually in the case of the sand wedge.

BRASSIE: The No. 2 wood.

BREAK: The sideways curving of a shot as it rolls on the green.

BUNKER: A sand hazard, commonly called a "trap."

BYE: Situation in match play where a competitor has no opponent, because of insufficient number of qualifiers, and thus advances automatically to next round of play.

CADDIE: Someone who carries a player's clubs, who may perform various other services, and who has the right to give advice to the player and his side.

CARRY: The distance between ball's original position and where it lands.

CAST: To uncock or straighten the wrists prematurely in the downswing.

CASUAL WATER: Any temporary accumulation of water not regarded as a water hazard.

CHIP SHOT: Short approach shot of low trajectory, usually involving minimal carry and maximum bounce and roll.

CLOSE LIE: Ball setting down in grass or otherwise close to ground's surface. Also called a "tight lie."

CLOSED FACE: Clubface aimed left of intended line at address or on impact. Also, a position during the swing that is likely to produce a closed face at impact.

CLOSED STANCE: Left foot closer than right foot to intended line of flight.

CLOSED ALIGNMENT: Positioning of left side closer than right side to intended line of flight.

CLUBFACE: Normal striking surface of the clubhead.

COLLAR: Grass around the edges of a green or hazard.

COURSE: The terrain over which play is permitted.

COURSE RATING: The score a zero handicap ("scratch") golfer should make when playing well under normal conditions, as determined by a golf association for figuring handicaps of those who play the course in question.

CUP: Metal or plastic lining fitted into the hole.

CUPPY: Lie in which the ball sets in a depression.

CUT SHOT: Stroke applying a clockwise spin to the ball that causes it to curve from left to right.

DIVOT: Turf uprooted by clubhead during the swing.

DOGLEG: A hole with a fairway that bends to the left or right.

DORMIE: Situation in match play wherein a player or a side is ahead by as many holes as remain to be played.

DOUBLE BOGEY: Two strokes over par on a hole.

DOUBLE EAGLE: Three strokes under par on a hole.

DOWN: The number of holes a player or a side is behind in a match.

DRAW: A shot that starts on the intended line and then curves slightly to the left.

DRIVE: Shot made with a driver from the teeing ground.

DRIVING IRON: Club with the approximate loft of a No. 1 iron.

DROP: The act of a player facing a hole being played, standing upright, and dropping his ball over his shoulder on occasions when allowed or required to do so by the Rules of Golf.

Dub: A bad shot. Also, a poor golfer.

Duck Hook: A shot that nosedives and curves abruptly to the left.

Duffer: A poor player. Also called a "hacker" or a "dub."

Eagle: Two strokes under par on a hole.

Explosion: See "blast."

Face: See "clubface."

Fade: A shot that starts on the intended line and then curves slightly to the right.

Fairway: Area between teeing ground and green that is regularly mowed and otherwise prepared with special care.

Feather: To hit an intentionally high shot that curves gently from left to right, and that stops quickly upon landing.

Finesse: To deliberately play other than a standard shot, in overcoming obstacles, weather, ground conditions, and the like. Also called "type" shots.

Flagstick: The marker in the hole on the green. Also called the "pin."

Flashing: Uncocking the wrists and flipping the clubhead with the hands early in the downswing.

Flat Lie: A more obtuse angle than normal between the sole and the shaft of a club.

Flat Plane: A characteristic of a swing that is less upright, or shallower, than normal.

Flight Path: See "intended line."

Follow-Through: The portion of the swing occurring after ball has left clubface.

Fore: Warning cry shouted to player(s) in danger of being struck by a shot.

Forecaddie: Person positioned down the fairway to spot and mark position of players' shots.

Forward Press: Slight movement of some part of the anatomy, usually the hands, more or less toward the target immediately prior to starting the backswing.

Four-Ball: Match in which two people play their better ball against the better ball of two others. (Frequently mislabelled "best-ball.")

Foursome: A match in which two golfers play against two others and each side plays one ball, stroking alternately. Also, in North America, the common term for a group of four players.

FREE DROP: A "drop" in which no penalty is incurred.

FRINGE: See "apron."

FROG HAIR: See "apron."

FRONT NINE: First nine holes of an 18-hole course.

GIMME: Slang term for a putt conceded to an opponent in match play.

GRAIN: Flat-lying grass, usually on a green, that tends to pull shots in the direction it lies.

GREEN: Closely-cut area of the course that contains the hole, cup, and flagstick.

GREENIES: A form of gambling in which all players pay a set amount to the one whose tee shot finishes on the green and closest to the hole.

GRIP: The covered portion of the clubshaft that is held in the hands. Also, the player's grasp of the club.

GROSS SCORE: Actual score shot on a hole, or for a round, with no handicap strokes deducted.

GROUND UNDER REPAIR: Area of work on the course designated for the allowance of a free drop outside that area.

HALF OR HALVE: A tied hole in match play.

HANDICAP: A number indicating a golfer's skill. Based on 85 percent (96 percent after December 31, 1975) of the average of the ten lowest differences, from his last 20 rounds, between his gross score and the rating of the course where it was shot.

HANDICAP STROKES: Shots deducted from a player's score to determine his or her standing in a stroke play competition. Or, shots deducted from the score of the higher handicap player on designated holes (see "stroke holes") in match play competition.

HANGING LIE: A ball at rest on a severe downslope.

HAZARD: A natural or man-made obstacle of sand or water in which certain privileges of play are prohibited, such as grounding the clubhead at address.

HEAD: The striking portion at the end of the club.

HEEL: The part of the clubface nearest that shaft. Also, a shot struck on this portion of the face.

HIGH SIDE: Area above the hole on a sloping green.

HOLE: Circular opening of 4¼-inch diameter in green into which ball is played.

HOLE-HIGH: A shot to a green that finishes even with the hole but off to one side.

HOLE-IN-ONE: First shot of a hole when it finishes in the cup. Also called an "ace."

HOLE OUT: To make a stroke that puts the ball into the cup.

HONOR: The right to shoot first from the tee, earned by scoring lowest on the previous untied hole.

HOOD: To decrease the effective loft of the clubface at address by tilting its top edge forward. Also sometimes used in referring to a closed clubface.

HOOK: A shot that curves from right to left as a result of the clubface looking to the left of its path of movement on impact, and thus imparting counterclockwise sidespin.

HOSEL: The part of an iron clubhead into which the shaft fits.

INSIDE-OUT: Clubhead movement across the intended line from left to right during impact.

INSIDE THE LINE: The area on player's side of the intended line as he or she addresses the ball and swings.

INTENDED LINE: The path along which a player plans for a shot to travel. Also called "target line."

INTERLOCK: Type of grip in which the left forefinger and right little finger intertwine.

IRONS: Clubs with heads made primarily of metal, but not including putters.

LAG: Putt played primarily to finish near hole rather than actually in it.

LAY BACK: The act of increasing the effective loft of the clubface by tilting its top edge backward.

LIE: The position of the ball in relation to its immediate surroundings. Also, the angle formed by the club's sole and shaft.

LINKS: A course laid out on linksland, the sandy soil deposited by receding ocean tides. (Today the term is often used synonymously for any golf course).

LIP: The edge of the hole. Also, a putt that rims the hole but stays out.

LOFT: The degrees at which a clubface lies back from vertical.

LOOSE IMPEDIMENT: Natural objects not fixed or growing and not adhering to the ball, such as stones, leaves, twigs, worms, and insects. Sand and loose soil are loose impediments only on the putting green.

LOW SIDE: Area below the hole on a slanted area of green.

LOOP: Shifting the hands outward or inward near the top of the back-swing so that the plane of the downswing becomes steeper or shallower than that of the backswing.

MASHIE: Iron club with the approximate loft of a No. 5 iron.

MATCH: A contest between two players, or a player and a side, or two sides, which is determined by the number of holes won or lost.

MATCH PLAY: Competition conducted under rules governing matches.

MEDAL: The lowest of all qualifying scores (derives from traditional prizes of medals awarded in amateur golf).

MEDALIST: The person with the lowest qualifying score.

MEDAL PLAY: Colloquialism for competition based on the total number of strokes taken. Correct usage is "stroke play."

MID-IRON: Iron club with the approximate loft of a No. 2 iron.

MULLIGAN: A second attempt at a shot, sometimes allowed in friendly games. Usually taken on the first tee. Not recognized by Rules of Golf.

NASSAU: Betting competition in which stakes are wagered on the out-come of the first nine holes, second nine holes, and the entire 18.

NECK: That part of any club where the shaft joins the head.

NET: Score for a hole or a round after handicap strokes are deducted.

NIBLICK: Club with the approximate loft of a No. 8 iron.

OBSTRUCTION: Anything on the course that is artificial, whether erected, placed, or left, except: (a) object defining out of bounds limits; (b) arti-ficial surfaces and side of roads and paths; (c) any construction deemed an integral part of the course by the local committee.

OPEN FACE: Clubface aimed right of intended line at address or on im-pact. Also refers to a clubface position during the swing that is likely to produce an open face at impact.

OPEN STANCE: Right foot closer than left to intended line of flight. Same applies to "open shoulders," "open hips," and the like.

OPEN TOURNAMENT: Competition in which both amateurs and pro-fessionals are eligible. Or any tournament conducted on an open entry rather than an invitational basis.

OUT OF BOUNDS: Area from which playing shots is disallowed.

OUT-OF-BOUNDS SHOT: Stroke that finishes in an out-of-bounds area. Shot must be replayed from original position, thus sacrificing distance gained, with one penalty stroke added.

OUTSIDE-IN: Clubhead movement across intended line from right to left during impact.

OUTSIDE THE LINE: The area on the opposite side of the intended target line as a player addresses the ball and swings.

OVER THE TOP: Incorrectly starting the downswing by turning the right shoulder around, as if throwing sidearm, instead of swinging it under. Generally causes outside-in clubhead path and ultra-steep angle of attack.

OVERLAP: Grip type in which right little finger laps over left forefinger. Popularized by the late Harry Vardon, thus also called "Vardon" grip.

PAR: Score an expert would be expected to make on a hole, including the allowance of two putts on the green.

PIN-HIGH: See "hole-high."

PITCH: Approach shot of high trajectory made with a highly-lofted club that settles relatively quickly upon landing.

PITCH-AND-RUN: Shot played with an iron so that it flies lower than normal and runs readily forward upon landing.

PITCHING WEDGE: Short-shafted iron club that is second only to sand wedge in its degree of loft.

PIVOT: The turning of the body during the swing.

PLAY THROUGH: An invitation given by a slower-playing group to let the following group go ahead by "playing through" as the slow group stands aside.

PLUGGED LIE: Ball at rest in the indentation it made upon landing.

PREFERRED LIES: Easing of the rules that allows player to move ball to a better position in the fairway when course conditions are substandard. Not recognized in Rules of Golf. Also called "winter rules."

PRESS: An extra bet, usually equal to the original amount, requested by a losing player. Also refers to an effort to gain extra distance by applying more force than necessary in swinging. (See also "forward press.")

PROVISIONAL BALL: A second ball played from the same spot as the original when the first ball is suspected of being lost or out of bounds.

PULL: A shot that travels more or less on a straight line but to the left of of the player's intended line.

PUNCH SHOT: An intentionally low shot resulting from the hands' leading the clubhead through impact and thus decreasing the club's effective loft.

PUSH: A shot that flies more or less straight but to the right of the player's intended line.

PUTT: Stroke made on the green with a putter.

PUTTER: Least-lofted club in the bag; usually used for rolling ball on the green.

PUTTING GREEN: See "green."

READING THE GREEN: Determining the line a shot—usually a putt—will seemingly take on the putting surface.

READING THE PUTT: See "reading the green."

RELEASE: The act of freely swinging the arms down and forward and uncocking the wrists without inhibition as the body unwinds.

RIM: The edge of the hole. Also, causing a ball to roll around the edge of the hole without falling in.

RHYTHM: The variation in speed of movement within one's swing. The "beat" of the swing within its overall pace or tempo.

ROUGH: Area of the course that is not considered fairway, green, or hazard; usually unmowed and relatively unkempt.

ROUND: The playing of the holes of a course in proper sequence. A "stipulated round" is 18 holes unless otherwise authorized by the local committee.

ROUND ROBIN: Competition in which every player or side competes against every other player or side once.

RUB OF THE GREEN: The occasion when a shot is stopped or deflected by an agency not part of the match or, in stroke play, part of the competitor's side. Also refers in general usage to any kind of bad luck.

SAND TRAP: Common term for "bunker." A hazard filled with sand.

SCOTCH FOURSOME: Common North American term for competition in which two partners play one ball, alternating strokes.

SCRATCH PLAY: Competition in which no handicap strokes are awarded.

SCRATCH PLAYER: Golfer with a handicap of zero.

SCUFF: To contact ground before the ball on one's forward stroke.

SETUP: See "address."

SHAFT: The elongated portion of the club to which the grip and clubhead are attached.

SHAFT FLEX: The built-in degree to which a shaft will bend under a given amount of pressure.

SHANK: A shot that flies to the right of the intended line, due to being contacted on the neck or hosel of the club rather than on the clubface.

SHORT GAME: Pitching, chipping, and putting.

SIDE: The player or players forming one part of a match.

SINGLE: A match between two players.

SKIN: See "syndicates."

SKULL: See "blade."

SKY: To mishit a shot so that the ball flies higher and shorter than expected.

SLICE: A shot that curves sharply from left to right of the intended line because of clockwise sidespin resulting from the clubface being open to the clubhead path during impact.

SOLE: The bottom of the clubhead. Also, the act of placing the club on the ground at address.

SPOON: The No. 3 wood.

SQUARE FACE: Clubface aimed down intended line at address or on impact. Also refers to a clubface position during the swing that is likely to produce a square face during impact.

SQUARE POSITION: A straightline relationship formed by the back of the left hand, wrist, and forearm.

SQUARE STANCE: Both feet equidistant from intended target line. Same applies to "square shoulders," and "square hips"—each equidistant from, or aligned parallel to, the intended target.

STIFF: Shot finishing very close to flagstick.

STONY: See "stiff."

STROKE: Forward movement of the club made with the intention of striking at and moving the ball.

STROKE HOLES: Holes on which, in match play, the higher handicap player or side receives a net score.

STROKE PLAY: Competition decided by the sum of the strokes taken by a player or his side.

SUDDEN DEATH: Additional competition played over extra holes until a winner is determined from among those tied at the end of regulation play.

SWINGWEIGHT: A measurement reflecting the weight distribution of a club's various components as determined on a swingweight scale. Used primarily for matching clubs within a set so that they feel the same when swung.

SYNDICATES: A form of gambling in which a set amount is paid by all players to the player who scores the lowest score on a hole.

TAKEAWAY: Initial part of the backswing.

TARGET LINE: An imaginary line extending from the golfer's target back to and through and beyond his ball.

TEE: The small peg on which the ball is usually set and from which it is played on the opening shot of the hole. (See also, "teeing ground.")

TEE SHOT: The first shot played on a hole.

TEEING GROUND: A rectangular area two club-lengths in depth, the front and sides of which are defined by the outside limits of two "tee" markers. Some portion of the ball must be within this area on all tee shots. Commonly called the "tee."

TEEING UP: The act of placing the ball on a tee. Sometimes used colloquially for the act of playing golf, as in "Let's tee it up."

TEMPO: The overall pace of a player's golf swing.

TEXAS WEDGE: Slang expression referring to the putter when used for shots from off the green.

THREE-BALL: A match in which three play against one another, each playing his own ball.

THREESOME: A match in which one plays against two, and each side plays one ball. Generally used in North America to designate a three-ball.

THROUGH THE GREEN: The whole area of the course except all of its hazards and the teeing ground and green of the hole being played.

TIMING: The sequence of movement of various parts of the body during the swing.

TOE: Part of the clubhead farthest from the shaft. Also, the act of contacting the ball with that portion of the clubhead.

TOP: Shot in which the leading edge or bottom of the club's sole contacts the ball above its center.

TRAP: See "sand trap." Also, the act of contacting the ball when the clubhead is still moving downward.

UPRIGHT LIE: A more acute angle than normal between the sole and the shaft of a club.

UPRIGHT PLANE: A characteristic of a swing that is steeper than normal.

UNPLAYABLE LIE: A ball not in a water hazard that is deemed unplayable by its owner because of its positioning.

VARDON GRIP: See "overlap."

WAGGLE: Clubhead movement at address prior to swinging.

WHIFF: A stroke in which the clubhead fails to make any contact with the ball.

WHIPPING: Thread or twine used to wrap the area where the head and shaft of the club join.

WINTER RULES: See "preferred lies."

WOODS: Clubs with heads made primarily of wood, excepting putters.